WHAT'S IN A WORD?

Webb Garrison

RUTLEDGE HILL PRESS®
Nashville, Tennessee

A Division of Thomas Nelson, Inc.
www.ThomasNelson.com

Published by Rutledge Hill Press, a division of Thomas Nelson, Inc., P.O. Box 141000, Nashville, Tennessee 37214.

Illustrations by Jason Shulman

Design by Harriette Bateman

Library of Congress Cataloging-in-Publication Data

Garrison, Webb B.
    What's in a word? / Webb Garrison.
      p. cm.
    Includes bibliographical references and index.
    ISBN 1-55853-811-9
     1. English language—Etymology. I. Title.

PE1574 .G29 2000
422—dc21

00–035288
CIP

Printed in the United States of America

03 04 05 — 7

CONTENTS

INTRODUCTION

SHORT SHORT STORIES

COBWEBS sometimes appear overnight, even in the best-kept quarters. These nuisances are such a common occurrence their name may seem prosaic. However, that is far from the case. In chapter 10 you will discover that a long-abandoned name for the spider is seen to have played a major role in the development of the word that now seems so ordinary.

Practically every word and phrase that we use is an easy-to-swallow verbal capsule. They're often potent and complex, being the end result of centuries of use. I have been fascinated by etymology (the study of word origins and developments) since my youth. I wrote brief word studies for the *Ladies' Home Journal*, which published three or four of them every month for years. One of the *Journal's* readers, who lived in what was then the Transvaal Africa, wrote to the editors of the magazine suggesting they publish the word studies together in a book. This led to a 1955 volume made up of reprinted material from *Ladies' Home Journal*, *Catholic Digest*, *Mechanix Illustrated*, *Better Homes and Gardens*, *Golf Digest*, *Elementary Electronics*, and other publications.

Like the previous book, this book is written in the form of "short short stories"—abbreviated forms of the American short story in which O. Henry excelled. The vignettes included here are brief enough for bathroom reading, and many of them include surprise endings almost, but not quite, in the fashion of Paul Harvey's tales.

The words and phrases in this book are divided into chapters on a somewhat arbitrary basis. Since it is intended for fun reading, the categories are mainly a way to segment the book. The index will help with reference use.

The words and phrases in this book were selected on the basis of interest, not because one is more significant and useful than another. Scholars who devote their whole lives to etymology have thick volumes dealing with words and phrases that are so complex it's difficult to follow their trails. Though they are an important aspect of our language, words and phrases of this sort are not included here. Everything here was selected for third millennial use. There are very new and very old words and phrases. Here's wishing you lots of fun, plus maybe a bit of learning!

Webb Garrison
Lake Junaluska, North Carolina—
in the heart of the Great Smokies

CHAPTER 1

HIGH TECHNOLOGY AND THE COMPUTER AGE

HIT	HACKER
THE TUBE / BOOB TUBE	TO BOOT
COMPUTER	FERRET
CURSOR	SPAM
MOUSE	CD-ROM
VIRUS	BULLET
ROBOT	ANTENNA
THE DOW	BYTE
CHIP	BROWSER
E-MAIL	BOOKMARK
FLOPPIES	BIT
GIG	

Hit

SOMEONE who connects with a target scores a hit. In baseball, players have distinguished between a hit in which the ball is "fair," within bounds, or a "foul ball," one that is out of bounds. A successful Broadway play, motion picture, television series, book, syndicated column, or comic strip character—along with many other things—is also dubbed a hit.

This ancient word soon came to designate a computer user's visit to a Web site. Since each such visit can be counted by means of a relatively simple program, the popularity—and hence the importance—of a Web site is measured in terms of how often a *hit* is registered in the course of a day, a week, or a month.

The Tube / Boob Tube

BEFORE the advent of flat screens and high definition television, all TVs functioned by means of a cathode ray tube. This factor, plus the shapes of early sets, fostered the use of the term *the tube* to designate a television set of any kind or size. Derogatory remarks about the quality of material seen on the tube prompted many Americans to begin sneering at the television, calling it *the boob tube*. Although digital television is sure to take over in the third millennium, such a tubeless set is likely to continue to be called *the tube*.

Computer

HUMANS were the earliest computers. These "counting persons" were professionals who worked with numbers and were credited with great accuracy. There is a nursery rhyme that talks about a king counting his money in his counting house. He was at the financial center of his kingdom where he almost certainly had computers doing the work. This early computing was manual and involved the use of such counting tools as the abacus and a variety of slide rules. When adding machines were developed, the man or woman who computed with one of these then-rapid devices often called the counting machine a computer. Used in this fashion, the hoary old term took on new life when it became attached to electronic data processing and storage devices.

Cursor

A LATIN term for "flowing" or "running" gave rise to the word "cursive" to describe handwriting produced in flowing style. The flow of letters that is produced when a pen is guided by skilled fingers is an impressive art. The name for this efficient and effortless writing style, in this computer age, soon was adapted and bestowed upon the small marker that moves quickly and gracefully across a computer screen. The *cursor* blinks until stimulated into action.

Mouse

A WEE rodent, usually brownish or grayish brown in color, abounds throughout the world. Its English name is derived from the same classical term that named the modern muscle—also small and often fast-moving. No known culture or civilization, ancient or modern, is known to have been without this creature.

Late last century engineers developed a little hand-held device used to control movements of a cursor. This device is small and rounded and has a cord that looks like a tail; hence, they called it a "mouse." Although the shapes have changed some over the years, the catchy name is likely to remain.

Virus

WHEN scientists first isolated a minute parasitic structure that causes serious illness, they called it a virus, which is Latin for "poison." Unable to live in isolation, a virus can reproduce with incredible speed when inside a suitable host organism such as a human body. When hackers and other computer enthusiasts who found out how to insert a small self-replicating program into a larger "host" program, the name was obvious: electronic *virus*. Such a set of data cannot travel or survive by itself but thrives as a parasite when it gets inside a computer. Like a submicroscopic particle of biochemistry, a computer virus can do great damage to any host in which it lodges, whether sent there deliberately or picked up accidentally.

Robot

THE Czech playwright Karel Capek was among the pioneers of twentieth-century science fiction. As part of his "black utopias," works showing the dangers of technological progress, he wrote a play called *R. U. R.* It centers on a group of mechanical monsters that revolt against their makers. Abbreviating a Czech term for a serf or slave, Capek used the word *robot* to designate the imaginary machine-man of his story. At the end, robots, who had been created to serve humans, came to dominate them completely. The term *robot* has now entered numerous languages.

The Dow

LONG ago executives at Dow Jones and Company saw a need for a formula to indicate upward and downward movements of the New York Stock Exchange. They selected thirty securities from industry, transportation, and utilities to form a workable base.

By the last decade of the twentieth century, the Dow Jones average has become simply *the Dow*. Since the Dow is tightly controlled by the owners of the name, it has been comparatively easy to modify the makeup of its components when changing industrial and economic conditions seem to warrant. For example, Sears, Roebuck and Company, a long-time component of the Dow, has been dropped, and Home Depot, Inc. has been added to the base list.

Regardless of how carefully those who control the Dow monitor its performance and make modifications to its thirty-corporation list, it can never be a comprehensively accurate indicator because thousands of corporations are not included in the average. Early in this millennium, hi-tech stocks skyrocketed, but most of them are not included in the Dow. A more accurate indicator is to check the movements of all securities traded on the market.

Nevertheless, investors worldwide watch the Dow more closely than any other index. Minute-by-minute media reports on gains or losses in the Dow are now so commonplace that it's hard to realize that these reports have become available only recently. They have strengthened the prestige of the venerable but less-than-exact barometer of action on the world's most influential stock exchange.

Chip

FOR centuries, a bit of wood or stone or metal that has been broken or cut off of a larger mass has been called a "chip." This old name became used to refer to thinly sliced wafers of potatoes, or potato chips. Other chips became popular around poker tables, roulette wheels, and many other games of chance.

During very recent decades silicon, which is the basic material of ordinary sand, was found to be a suitable material for making small wafers of semiconductor material. Once it became possible to manufacture this new kind of *chip* in quantity at low cost, the computer industry in California's Silicon Valley became a major site of its manufacture.

E-mail

THE transmission of messages by government-operated and private mail services helped to usher the Western world into the technological age. First letters and packages moved by surface mail, followed by telegrams, telephone messages, and airmail. Yet the old term for material sent through a postal system did not experience radical changes until hi-tech instruments became commonplace and inexpensive.

Development of recording devices that can be attached to telephones produced voice mail—now omnipresent, and a nuisance to some. Once it became possible for one computer to communicate with another computer, electronic mail surged into prominence. Strictly speaking, e-mail should be called something else since it doesn't flow through a postal system. New as the terminology is, however, academicians aren't likely to affect the increasingly important role of *e-mail*.

Floppies

THE development of a way to store data and to retrieve it from a small plastic disk with a magnetically coated surface revolutionized the personal computer. Early disks were thin, comparatively large, and pliable. As a result, it was natural to describe them as being "floppy."

Soon floppy disks were supplanted by a smaller and thicker magnetic disk whose width was only 3.25 inches, with its length a trifle longer. This 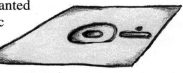 type of disk is now more familiar than the Latin *discus* that named many kinds of round, flat objects. Although computer disks are now encased in rigid plastic, they retain the name of their predecessors and are called *floppies*.

Gig

OUR earliest ancestors probably spent hundreds of generations learning to count as many objects as there were fingers on their hands. Even then, mastery of the abstract concept "ten" lay far in the future. Gradually moving upward in mathematical ability, humans learned to deal with hundreds and then with thousands. The ability to think or calculate in terms of millions came a great deal later.

Now, in the third millennium, the capacity to store, retrieve, and transmit electronic information has required another giant mathematical step, since it's commonplace to think and to act in terms of billions of data units. The abbreviation of the classical Greek term for "gigantic" made it customary to use "giga" to indicate a binary billion, or ten to the ninth power. With the final letter dropped, it became a *gig*.

The development of gigabyte-capacity storage disks—actually equivalent to 1,024 megabytes—is now taken for granted. This usage represents a radical departure from that of labeling an engagement by a musician or group of musicians a "gig," since such a one-time booking might be anything but large in terms of audience or pay.

Hacker

FOR centuries the verb "hack" has meant the action of cutting or chopping anything from stove wood to enemy soldiers by means of a series of short blows delivered by an ax, a sword, or some other blade.

Only a fraction of present-day Americans regularly go out to hack wood into pieces small enough to be burned in a stove. Hi-tech weapons have made battle-axes, swords, sabers, and all other sharp-edged hand-wielded weapons obsolete. Yet the number of persons who spend time delivering repeated blows to electronic systems in order to understand or infiltrate them appears to be growing.

Today's *hacker* may spend days or weeks repeatedly striking a computer system for purposes of harm, mischief, or simple curiosity.

Dedicated perseverance and use of the brain make a "hacker" a force to be reckoned with in the modern world.

To Boot

THE phrase "pulled himself up by his bootstraps" is used admiringly to describe a self-made success. Drawing only on his or her own inner resources, without help from any outside source, this person has made a mark in life.

Early computer programmers faced an obstacle: the memories of their computers were wiped clean each time the machines were turned off. To address this problem, the programmers needed to enter a short program called a "bootstrap loader" each time the machine was turned on. Once this program was read, the computer could then perform more complex functions. The short program gave the machine a "bootstrap" it could then use to perform tasks; without it, the computer was useless.

Over time, programmers figured out ways to design software so computers could perform this function automatically, and bootstrap loaders are now part of the basic makeup of any operating system. Pulling oneself up by the bootstrap is a means of restarting one's situation. The expression lives on in the phrase *to boot,* which today simply means to turn on, but reflects decades of efforts of computer programmers to make computers easier to use.

Ferret

A WEASEL-LIKE, usually albino, mammal related to the polecat has long been trained to hunt rabbits and other small game. Called a "ferret," from the Latin word for "little thief," the rodent is persistent in its efforts to steal its quarry.

Relatively small Internet search engines that operate extremely fast became popular late last millennium. Today, a *ferret* may scurry through masses of electronic data and nearly always succeeds in "stealing" a desired tidbit of information.

Spam

EXECUTIVES at the Hormel Foods Corporation, one of the world's foremost meat packers, had a brainstorm in the middle of the twentieth century. Seeking a catchy trade name that could be registered, Hormel offered a one hundred dollar prize to the person who could come up with the best name for its canned minced pork product. The winner came up with the name "Spam."

Spam, still stocked on supermarket shelves everywhere, played a major but little-known role in world events. Nikita Khrushchev paid a special visit to company headquarters in Minnesota to express his personal thanks for the role Spam played in feeding Russian soldiers during World War II, and American GIs will never forget this staple of their undesirable C rations.

Although it may have sustained many soldiers during World War II, after the war Spam got a reputation for being "junk" meat. In the early days of the Internet vendors began experimenting with advertising through brief messages sent to multitudes of computer users. The popular name for the famous meat packers' "junk" meat soon came to refer to this unwanted, or "junk," e-mail.

CD-ROM

AS an abbreviation, this cluster of letters has come to function as a word naming a compact disc crammed with an immense amount of data, graphic material, music, or other sounds. The disc can be read or viewed and printed out but can't be altered, making deletion of selected portions impossible. Once the basic nature of this disc is understood, it makes complete sense that the abbreviation stands for Compact Disc [with] Read-Only Memory — *CD-ROM.*

Bullet

WHEN early printers wished to highlight a particular passage, they put a heavy dot beside it. This dot resembled the round projectile fired from a pistol or musket, so they called it a bullet.

Computer software enables a user to put a marker of selected size, shape, and color at a desired point in a file or document. A *bullet* of this sort gives no hint that its earliest ancestor was used in combat.

Antenna

ANCIENT Roman sailors hung their sails from a horizontal arm, or yard, which they called an antenna. Eventually the nautical term came to designate horns, or feelers, of insects that resemble yards of a ship.

The development of sound transmission without use of wires required the invention of receiving devices, many of which had a superficial resemblance to an insect's antenna. Although today's technology has made it possible to eliminate them from many devices, the word *antenna* remains alive and well as a designation for receiving gear that is essential to weather cubes and countless numbers of radios and radio-controlled devices.

Byte

WHEN computers were rare and very expensive, users of binary notation modified and combined binary and digit to form the name for a cluster of eight adjoining bits designating a letter or numeral such as *g* or *9*. Though wholly artificial, *byte* has entered scores of languages and is one of the few words that is likely to have the same meaning regardless of where it is encountered.

Browser

TURNED loose in a lush grass-covered field, nearly every horse, cow, or other domestic animal will move from one especially tender clump of grass to another, browsing through the field. The term "browser" came to be applied to a shopper flitting from one spot in a store to another or to a reader picking a page here and a page there in a book.

Today's most frequent *browser* is neither an animal nor a person. Instead, it's computer software designed for incredibly fast "picking and choosing" from many spots on the World Wide Web. This high-tech browser offers a choice of sites that promises— maybe—to have the clump of information for which the user is searching.

Bookmark

DURING the infancy of printed books, users didn't like to risk damage by turning pages unnecessarily. Instead, they used slips of leather, fabric, or paper to mark their place. The aristocracy and those in some monastic orders used extremely elaborate bookmarks that took scores of man-hours to produce.

With a single keystroke, today's computer users can insert a bookmark at any desired point in a word-processed document or a CD-ROM. Marked in such a fashion, a word or paragraph can be accessed almost instantly without opening a book or turning a single page.

Bit

DERIVED from the Middle English word for "morsel," the word "bite" came to mean the amount of food one could take into the mouth at one time—not a large amount. Soon abbreviated to "bit," the modified name also came to designate a small device put into the mouth of a horse. In the very early sense, "bit" came to be applied to anything that was small in size. The term *bit* is also used to describe the smallest unit of code (expressed either as *0* or *1*) that can be stored in a computer. The word, however, was derived from the combined words "*b*inary dig*it*." Considering the evolution of the word "bite" and its designation of small things, it is no wonder that the computer scientists chose the letters they did to abbreviate the smallest unit of binary code.

CHAPTER 2

SPORTS AND RECREATION

UPSHOT

STYMIED

ROOKIE

HANDS DOWN

WELL HEELED

UNDERHANDED

UMPIRE

BESIDE THE MARK

CIRCUS

HAND RUNNING

RAISE THE HACKLES

RING THE BELL

AT THE END OF ONE'S ROW

PLANK DOWN

COME UP TO SCRATCH

ABOVEBOARD

RIGHT DOWN MY ALLEY

PAY THE PIPER

LEFT IN THE LURCH

FIRST-STRING

ON THE BALL

WANDER FROM PILLAR
TO POST

DERBY

HANDICAP

BANGS

KIBITZER

CHECKMATE

BACKBITE

AIREDALE

IN THE GROOVE

RINGLEADER

DOLL

BEST BIB AND TUCKER

CHIME IN

SPENDTHRIFT

Upshot

VILLAGERS of medieval Britain took their archery seriously. Big matches were gala affairs, affecting the social standing of every man who took part. Many were conducted like modern sports events; the fellow who won a given round moved up to the next. It wasn't unusual for competitors to be so closely matched that the last arrow shot of a round would determine its outcome.

In such circumstances a single arrow caused one man to drop out and the other to move up toward a new opponent. *Upshot* came to name the shot that could raise an archer up to a new round. Used by Shakespeare and Milton the sporting word entered general speech to signify any result or conclusion, no matter how remote from activities on the village green.

Stymied

GAMES somewhat like golf have been played since antiquity. It was in Scotland, however, that the modern sport took form. As early as 1450 it had become a craze with Highlanders. It interfered with archery so seriously that rulers handed down three separate edicts forbidding golf—in 1457, 1471, and 1491.

Public interest was too keen, however, and the law couldn't be enforced. Although golf spread to nearly all civilized lands, some of its most distinctive terms have Scottish origins. "Styme," an ancient term for "obscure" or "hidden," was used in the situation where one ball hides the cup from another.

When a player is stymied, he must choose between losing a stroke and trying to loft his ball over that of his opponent. As early as 1850 it was considered bad form to bring about a stymie on purpose. From the unplanned dilemma on the putting green, a person blocked in any effort is said to be *stymied*.

Rookie

WHETHER he is a pitcher, fielder, or baseman, the *rookie* owes his odd name to a long and tangled chain of circumstances. Rural folk of medieval England were greatly interested in a common type of crow known as a rook. These big birds nested in colonies and were loud, dirty, and generally disagreeable. Since they frequently occupied the same nest for years, a large rookery was likely to be cluttered with string, bits of cloth, shiny pebbles, and other stolen trinkets.

Farmers, often victimized at the county fair, compared human swindlers with these noisy feathered thieves. A person taken to the cleaners by a gang of rooks was laughingly called a "rookie." Since he was likely to be young and guileless, the word came to mean any novice or simple fellow. *Rookie* was eventually adopted by sportsmen in the United States as the designation for a raw beginner in professional baseball, later any professional sport.

Hands Down

PLANTATION owners and merchant princes of colonial America took great interest in horse racing. For many generations major contests were supported largely by the wealthy. After the Civil War promoters began bidding for attendance by the general public. Racing then surged to new popularity and prominence.

Skilled jockeys made an art of timing the final spurt toward the ribbon. Sometimes a fellow would be so far ahead of the field that he didn't have to lift his hands in order to urge his mount forward. Expecting an easy victory, the backer of a horse would boast that his jockey would win *hands down*. Erupting from racetrack lingo about the turn of the last century, the phrase came to indicate any effortless triumph.

Well Heeled

FIGHTING cocks, long the most prized of game animals, still have a high mortality rate. During the late Middle Ages it was unusual for any defeated fowl to leave the pit alive. Owners of the birds usually fought them with the understanding that there would be no decision until one of the combatants fell dead.

Great care went into the breeding of birds. Occasionally a fowl would show every indication of being a superb fighter, but by an accident of nature he would have very short spurs or no spurs at all. In such instances it became customary to equip him with a metal spur or gaff. Strapped to the heels of fighters, these spurs were dangerous weapons. Owners began using them even when a cock had spurs of his own. Craftsmen vied with one another in devising artificial heels of iron, brass, or even silver. A bird so equipped was said to be *well heeled*—or armed for a fight to the death.

Cockfighting waned in popularity a few centuries ago but was revived around 1875, when it quickly won many enthusiasts. Toughs and rowdies who frequented the cockpits were open in their admiration of vicious heeled birds. It was natural that a fowl's weapon should be compared with a revolver, so that a person with a gun in his possession came to be described as "heeled." The term has been broadened. Now anyone who has plenty of fighting resources in the form of money is called *well heeled*.

Underhanded

PLAYING cards have been around for centuries, but it wasn't until the sixteenth century that they became popular in England. Once the little pasteboards became well known, they swept all other games of chance before them. Noblemen, merchants, soldiers, and artisans began to play at every opportunity.

It was inevitable that rogues should take advantage of beginners. By manipulating a few important cards under his hand, the dealer could control the game. Such *underhanded* play brought easy money to so many sharpers that by 1575 the term had come into general use to designate stealthy conduct at the card table or anywhere else.

Umpire

RUDE athletic contests were in great vogue among rough tribesmen who swarmed through western Europe after the fall of the Roman Empire. Since they were violent and often bloody, such games were staged between teams matched as evenly as possible. Every man on one side had a specific opponent on the other.

Disputes sometimes arose. In order to settle them with a minimum of violence, a nonparticipant was chosen as judge. Since he wasn't matched against an opponent, the judge was treated as an odd man—that is, not paired or "unpaired." Crossing the Channel with the Normans who conquered Britain in the eleventh century, the old sporting term emerged into modern speech as *umpire*.

Beside the Mark

IN medieval England, every village had its green where yeomen gathered for archery practice. This was the national pastime that produced skilled bowmen for military use.

For a target, the medieval marksmen used a bit of cloth or leather attached to a tree. Arrows that missed this mark or hit the tree *beside the mark* reduced an archer's score. Villagers took their competition so seriously that the bowman's term entered general speech to designate anything irrelevant or not to be counted.

Circus

NO other ancient people were more fond of parades, public games, and festivals than were the Romans. Among landmarks of the empire's capital was a huge arena flanked by rising tiers of seats. Because it was shaped somewhat like a *circus* or circle, the big edifice was called the *Circus Maximus* or "largest circle."

Centuries later many long-forgotten Latin words were resurrected. Among these was the ancient term for a sports arena, which was used to designate any large entertainment place. Gradually the name shifted from the building to the performances staged in it. Barnum added acrobats and jugglers to traditional equestrian acts, and the modern traveling *circus* was born.

Hand Running

MEDIEVAL Englishmen used "run" to stand for such diverse things as the path or track of an animal, a ravel in knitted fabric, and a course of good or bad luck in a game of chance. In the latter sense gamblers spoke of "a good run with the dice."

Around the middle of the seventeenth century, card playing became all the rage, and terminology of other games carried over. When a player received a number of good cards in a single deal, he spoke of getting them "in the run of a hand." This phrase implied quick succession, so *hand running* came to designate any group of things which follow one another rapidly or consecutively.

Raise the Hackles

MEDIEVAL householders made wide use of flax, whose fibers are so tough they had to be carefully worked with a tool called the *hackle*. Farmers noticed that angry fowls have a way of raising the feathers on their necks. Disturbed in such fashion, a bird looked as though someone had rumpled his feathers with a hackle. Hence by 1450 such feathers had taken the name of the combing tool.

Since visible hackles indicated anger, it was natural to say that anything causing an outburst of rage *raised the hackles* of the offended person.

Ring the Bell

AROUND 1890 strength-testing machines became popular. Every fair, circus, and carnival boasted several of them. Models differed in their particulars but all were equipped with a bell. When a person exhibited enough strength, he would cause the bell to ring. This helped attract other customers and was usually rewarded by a prize. Traveling shows carried these devices into every part of the country. They became so familiar that *to ring the bell* came to stand for success in any sort of effort.

At the End of One's Row

A PERSON who has exhausted his resources is likely to describe himself as *at the end of his row*. This usage links the phrase with hopelessness. Originally, however, it had quite a different connotation.

Cotton planters before the Civil War found the flat land of the South ideal for their operations. Especially in the river bottoms of Mississippi, Alabama, and parts of South Carolina, a field might stretch for hundreds of yards without a break or turn. Human labor was used for the tedious task of chopping cotton, and foremen found it easier to supervise workers in fields with long, straight rows.

Vigorous slaves, commonly called hands, frequently made a spurt as they neared the end of a row in order to win a few minutes of relaxation while laggards caught up with them. This practice was so general that a person who ceased effort of any sort was described as being *at the end of his row*. Eventually the phrase was linked with exhaustion and acquired its present meaning. The sailors' term, "at the end of one's rope," is nearly identical in sound and has the same significance.

Plank Down

PROFESSIONAL gamblers have always thrived on patrons of wandering fairs and shows. Especially in rural areas it's still not uncommon for a victim to become excited and play until his pockets are empty. Hoping for a change in luck, such a fellow is likely to ask for one more chance on credit.

This practice was especially prevalent around the turn of the nineteenth century, when many communities had not adopted laws to cover the country fair. Many games were crooked, and con men didn't give suckers a chance. They were too smart to permit credit, and when it was requested, they would refuse to play until all wagers were on the plank. "If you want in, mister," the operator would say, *"plank down."* Spread by word of mouth, the expression entered general speech as a command to produce cash—whether on a plank gambling rig or somewhere else.

Come Up to Scratch

WHEN prize fighting became popular in the seventeenth century, there were few rules. Bouts ordinarily lasted many hours, and padded gloves would have been scorned as effeminate. Noblemen began sponsoring fighters and bet heavily on them. Because thousands of pounds might depend on the outcome of a bout, sponsors would push their man out as long as he could stumble to his feet. The death rate became so high that the bruisers themselves insisted upon some rudimentary rules.

It became the custom to scratch a line on the ground and require fighters to stand with their toes on the line at the beginning of each round. A mauler unable to "come up to scratch" lost the bout. This earliest version of the technical knockout made so strong an impression on the general public that *come up to scratch* entered common speech as an expression for meeting requirements or qualifications of any nature.

Aboveboard

FROM the beginning of organized horse racing, gamblers and confidence men followed the track. A standard attraction at a medieval race was a crude gambling wheel, the forerunner of the roulette wheel. This device was customarily mounted on a stand, the sides of which were draped with gaily colored cloth.

Unscrupulous operators would install a treadle under the stand to regulate the stopping point of the wheel. Though the racket was exposed, it continued to flourish. A gambler who wished to impress on bystanders the honesty of his game would point to his wheel and cry, "All above the board, sirs! All above the board!" This claim that there was no concealed treadle under the board soon entered common speech as *aboveboard,* meaning "straightforward" or "without concealment."

Right Down My Alley

IN English usage an alley was originally a walkway. Later the meaning expanded to include any narrow passage, such as that between houses in a city or rows in a farmer's field. With the development of baseball, the term "alley" came to stand for imaginary lines running between the outfields. A ball hit straight down such an alley is comparatively hard to field and is likely to yield a home run.

Early sluggers liked to brag that they had alleys which practically belonged to them. Any easily hit ball was said by such a batter to be *right down my alley.* Spreading from the baseball diamond, the expression came to be applied to any undertaking especially suited to one's talents.

Pay the Piper

STREET dancing was a chief form of amusement during medieval times. However, not every flute player could pipe for a dance, so there developed a class of strolling musicians who would play for a dance wherever they could gather a crowd.

Frequently a dance was organized on the spur of the moment. Persons who heard the notes of a piper would drop their work and join in the fun. When they tired of the frolic, they would pass the hat and take up a collection for the musician. It became proverbial that a dancer had better have his fun while he could; sooner or later he would have to *pay the piper*.

Left in the Lurch

WHEN a person is hopelessly outdistanced, his rivals are likely to declare that they have *left him in the lurch*—using an odd expression born in competition.

Socialites of the sixteenth century often played the game lurch, which was somewhat like backgammon, and large sums of money were frequently at stake. After a time lurch went out of fashion and was no longer played, but its name passed into the lingo of other games to designate a state in which one competitor remains far behind. In cribbage, for example, lurch exists when a player has fewer than thirty-one points when his rival scores sixty-one.

Spreading from the gaming table, the expression took on new vigor. It became proverbial that a person *left in the lurch* was not a contender for a prize or honor.

First-String

FIRST-STRING" and "second-string," expressions familiar on every athletic field, originated when archery was the chief sport. Around the thirteenth century the five-foot English longbow became the world's most formidable weapon. At Abergavenny in 1182 a Welsh archer using a longbow of yew shot an arrow through a four-inch oak slab. Ordinary armor was no defense against it.

Royal proclamations urged adoption of the weapon, and in 1363 Edward III made it mandatory for men to engage in contests with the longbow on every Sunday and holiday.

These meets were the chief sporting events of the times, and every man coveted a prize. Much of the marksman's success lay in the use of a good bowstring. Although an archer usually had several strings, he invariably had a favorite that he considered superior to his others. In Old English speech this was his "fyrst-streng." When firearms made the longbow obsolete, the expression for one's finest bowstring became attached to the best squad in any group of contestants, so "secounde-streng" was a logical successor to *first-string*.

On the Ball

IN the entire history of sport, no other game has even approached the rapidity with which baseball skyrocketed to popularity. The first match game ever played took place at Hoboken, New Jersey. Enthusiasts of the new sport soon discovered that in it, the pitcher plays a far more important role than the pitcher in the British game of rounders from which baseball developed. American hurlers soon learned that they could deceive unwary batters by spinning the ball. After a particularly effective curve, skillful pitchers were said by their admirers to have something *on the ball*. This expression was so apt that it quickly came to stand for effectiveness in general.

Wander From Pillar to Post

THOUGH the ancients played games with racquets and balls, modern tennis probably developed in fifteenth-century France. Quickly crossing the channel, the sport became very popular in

England. Space was at a premium within great walled estates, so few tennis courts were built. Most gentlemen who took up the game played in their courtyards. It was natural that the front door of the castle should mark one side of the court, the entrance gate in the surrounding wall the other. A fast game, therefore, kept players moving from pillars of the mansion to posts of the gate.

Players and observers noticed this and adopted to *wander from pillar to post* as an expression for being driven from one difficulty to another.

Derby

ENGLAND has few families whose blood is a deeper shade of blue than that of the Stanleys. Descended from an aide of William the Conqueror, this family came into possession of the earldom of Derby in the fifteenth century. Their name entered common speech because the twelfth earl was a lover of fast horses. With no specific desire for fame, Derby established an annual race for three-year-old horses. First run in 1780, it quickly became the most noted race in England.

American sportsmen who took in the races after the Civil War were impressed by the odd hats some of the English spectators wore. They brought a few of the "Derby hats" back to the United States, where a new model was developed. Made of stiff felt with a dome-shaped crown and narrow brim, the derby won the heart of the American male. By the time the first Kentucky Derby was run in 1875, the *derby* was standard wear for the man of parts. It is merely incidental that the hat also brought a kind of immortality to the distinguished house of Derby.

Handicap

SIXTEENTH-CENTURY English gamblers had little equipment for organized games of chance. Playing cards were available only to the wealthy, and dice were scarce and expensive. Ordinary fellows therefore developed a gambling game that required no equipment but a hat or cap. A fellow wishing to get up a game would offer to trade some article with an acquaintance. For example, he might suggest exchanging his hood for another's cloak. Since no two articles were of identical worth, traders would select an umpire to decide the cash difference.

All three men dropped forfeit money into a cap, and the traders held their hands over the money. Then the umpire announced his decision concerning the difference in the value of the articles involved. With their eyes closed, the hagglers removed their hands from the cap—fists open or closed to indicate acceptance or refusal of the umpire's terms. If both agreed to trade or not to trade, forfeit money went to the umpire; otherwise, it went to the man who accepted the umpire's decision. Each of the three men stood to lose two ways and win in only one way, so a fellow with a "hand in cap" took considerable risk.

Then horse racers began using umpires to stipulate weights to be carried, and the term was shortened from "hand in cap" to *handicap*. By the eighteenth century the meaning had expanded to include any type of weight, encumbrance, disadvantage, or disability.

Bangs

ECONOMIC disturbances in the middle of the nineteenth century played havoc with many rich sportsmen. Some of them had to sell their stables. Others merely reduced their staff and kept their animals. Shorthanded stable bosses found it impossible to groom the horses as carefully as they had in the past. Instead of spending the customary hours in trimming the tail of an animal, the groomers whacked the tail off square, or "bang off."

Bangtail animals won several major races and attracted wide attention. Designers took note, and by the third quarter of the century, many fashionable women were wearing their hair in *bangs*.

Kibitzer

IN the eyes of cardplayers kibitzers are the lowest form of humanity. Though not playing themselves, they give frequent advice, peering at the cards of one player, then another. Their name is derived from *kibitz*, a German word for the lapwing or plover. This bird characteristically jabbers incessantly but cannot sing. By its shrill cry it frightens game away upon the approach of hunters and generally makes a nuisance of itself.

German card players of the 1500s likened the comments of these onlookers to the chattering of the kibitz. The name stuck, passed into many languages, and serves as a perpetual reminder that the *kibitzer* can be a very annoying bird.

Checkmate

FEW expressions have a more ancient lineage than "checkmate." Now synonymous with "to thwart" or "to frustrate," it was long restricted to the game of chess.

No one knows where chess originated or when. It was already old when early Arabs borrowed it from the Persians. Through Spanish traders it reached Europe in the eighth century. In taking up the new game, the West adopted some of the ancient terms connected with it.

One such word was *shah* (king), designating the most important of the playing pieces. According to rules of the game, when one's shah was trapped, defeat was inevitable. An Arab who maneuvered his opponent into a hopeless position would cry, *Shah mat!* (The king is dead!) Passing through Spanish and French, this expression entered English as *checkmate* and came to name any stroke of victory.

Backbite

MEDIEVAL Europe had few sports as popular as bearbaiting. An animal that was captured as a cub would be trained to fight dogs. Then the bear's owner would take him from village to village and set him against the dogs of local sporting men. These fights usually took place in some public place and constituted community outings. No admission was charged, but the bear's master would take up a collection some time during the exhibition.

Rough though the sport was, a few rules grew up to govern it. For example, the bear's master was required to fasten him to a post with a chain which could not exceed an agreed length. Owners of dogs were expected to keep their animals in hand and to let only a few attack the bear at once.

When a bear was pulled up short by reaching the end of his chain, some of the dogs would hold him at bay. Sometimes one of the pack would slip behind the bear and attack him from the rear. Unable to protect himself from such a *backbite*, the bear would let out a roar of pain and rage. Good sportsmanship outlawed the backbite, but it was a common occurrence. As early as the twelfth century the term had come to describe anyone taking an unfair advantage. Then its meaning expanded, and the expression entered modern speech to mean speaking ill of a person behind his back.

Airedale

UNDER English law the right to hunt wild animals was restricted to landowners until 1831. Though game was plentiful in the great forests, ordinary folk were not permitted to take it, even for food. As a result poaching flourished. Severe penalties didn't stop the practice; they only made trespassing hunters more wary.

Professional poachers bred special terriers with keen noses, good fighting ability, and of a color difficult to see at night. Such animals were bred in West Yorkshire, in the dale or valley of the River Aire. Hence, the poacher's dog was called an *Airedale*. Kennel clubs became interested in the breed around 1850, and for years it was one of the most popular strains used by legitimate hunters.

In the Groove

THOMAS Edison's first talking machine, made from a brass pipe into which spiral grooves had been cut, was a scientific marvel when it was patented in 1877. Tinfoil wrapped over the brass was indented by sound impressions and reproduced the sound with some fidelity. Everything went well so long as the clumsy needle remained in the groove. When the needle jumped from its place, pandemonium resulted.

A modified apparatus using a wax cylinder soon came on the market and was admired by all who heard it. But every operator was cautioned to keep the needle *in the groove,* and in time the phrase came to label any kind of good performance.

Ringleader

DANCING was a major recreational device in medieval Europe. There were few commercial amusements, so many folks in the communities turned out for dances.

A majority of popular folk dances began with all participants holding hands in a circle. At a signal the circle was broken, and one person or couple would lead the rest of the ring through traditional figures. A skillful *ringleader* had a place of honor and was very much in demand at social functions of all sorts. Consequently, the dancer's title expanded and is now used to label anyone who leads others—especially if they are engaged in informal or illicit activities.

Doll

RURAL folk of medieval England were prone to the traditions of their ancestors, even in such matters as personal names. An estimated 90 percent of men and women at the time had one of a dozen or so names. Among the most popular female names was "Dorothy," meaning literally, "gift of God." However, the popular inclination has always been to substitute nicknames. Thus girls named Dorothy were often called "Doll." By the sixteenth century it had degenerated into a term for a loose woman, a "play thing." From there the word *doll* was transferred to the name of a child's toy, representing a human being.

Best Bib and Tucker

LATE in the 1600s, a fashionable dress style for women featured a long, full skirt and a low-necked bodice, short-waisted with a short peplum, which resembled a baby's bib. Often the women tucked a bit of lace into the top of the bodice.

When a woman wished to make a particularly stunning impression, she naturally wore her *best bib and tucker*. Adopted into common speech, the expression came to stand for any stylish outfit—whether worn by women or men.

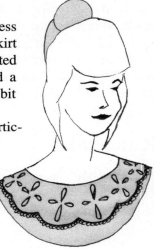

Chime In

SOME time before the fourteenth century, a way to ring the bells or chimes in a church tower has been for a simple melody to be played by striking them, with other bells echoing it.

Conversations sometimes resembled the music from a cathedral tower. A person of importance would give his opinion, and others in the group would mumble agreement. Thus a person who merely echoed another's opinion was said to *chime in*.

Spendthrift

COMMON folk of medieval Europe were frequently taxed at a rate which makes our income tax seem mild. As a result it was difficult for any except noblemen to accumulate an estate. When a man did succeed in saving money to be left to his sons, he proudly referred to it as his "thrift." Some heirs dissipated the thrift of a lifetime in short order. As a result *spendthrift* entered the language as a vivid expression for any type of prodigal.

CHAPTER 3

LEGAL TALK

CHARACTER

JURY

BRING TO BOOK

ALIAS

ON THE SPOT

JUG

CORONER

SUBPOENA

CHEAT

RIGMAROLE

TRIAL

RAG

ALCATRAZ

BEAT THE RAP

JURY OF TWELVE

KANGAROO COURT

POSSE

BURGLAR

BLACKMAIL

JAILBIRD

LEAN OVER
 BACKWARD

VILLAIN

Character

ROMAN artisans, highly skilled in working with some kinds of metal, developed a special tool for stamping and marking. The name of this tool passed through Old French into English as "character." Centuries of usage made the word come to stand for both the tool and the mark produced by it.

Medieval courts used a character to brand a convicted lawbreaker so that person could never again pass as an upright citizen. The letter *A* was burned upon a woman guilty of adultery; the letter *M* marked a murderer sentenced to penal servitude; and the letter *T* was burned upon the forehead or shoulder of a thief.

Anyone branded with such a symbol was marked for life. One glance at his "character" was sufficient to tell a stranger what he was, so by the sixteenth century, *character* had come to stand for the sum total of one's qualities.

Jury

THE legal processes of twelfth-century England were often informal. If someone seized a subject's property, the victim could buy a royal writ from the king to assure a hearing. The official presiding over the hearing would assemble a group of twelve neighbors who knew the facts of the case. Since the French-speaking Normans then ruled the island kingdom, the men who had to swear, or *jurer,* an oath to tell the truth came to be known as a *jury.* These "sworn" men reached a decision on the basis of personal knowledge related to the case. Lawyers later adopted the use of sworn citizens who relied on the evidence of others, and the modern jury came into being.

Bring to Book

SINCE ancient times persons brought before courts of law have been required to attest to their sincerity. Ceremonies varied widely through the centuries but were standardized late in the

Middle Ages. It became customary for a witness to place his hand on the Bible at the same time he took an oath to answer questions truthfully.

This practice stemmed from the belief in the power of the sacred Book. It was believed that after swearing upon the Bible a fellow could be struck dead if he lied! It became proverbial that if a law-breaker could be brought to the Book, he would admit his guilt and accept his punishment. Criminals eventually lost their superstitious fear of the Holy Writ, but *bring to book* remains a synonym for "compel an explanation or an accounting."

Alias

SCHOLARS of medieval England developed great pride in their learning. A "man of letters" seldom used ordinary language. Instead he relied almost entirely upon Latin.

Lawyers were fond of displaying their knowledge and frequently used Latin phrases, even in their courtroom addresses. One such expression was *alias dictus,* meaning "otherwise called." A criminal known by more than one name might be mentioned as Richard Stone, *alias dictus* Robert Scott. Use of the sonorous phrase was so frequent that by 1535 ordinary folk had adopted the word *alias* to designate any assumed name.

On the Spot

POLICE courts of the past and present have often disregarded the legal rights of prisoners. Officers in charge of such courts have sometimes used every possible means to secure a confession from a suspect. Open brutality prevailed until the latter part of the nineteenth century when aroused public opinion led violent methods of "questioning" to become illegal.

As a substitute for violence, mental and physical ordeals were devised. One of these methods consisted of forcing a suspect to stand on "the spot"—a tiny square marked with chalk. Without permitting a prisoner to move from the spot, officers would bombard him with accusations for hours. While forced to remain *on the spot,* it was dangerous to say anything, yet the accused couldn't ignore all of the questions fired at him. Borrowed from police jargon, the phrase came to name the state of being in any delicate or dangerous position.

Jug

A JAIL or prison is sometimes referred to as "the jug." Though widely thought to be pure slang, the expression has an ancient and honorable lineage.

Long before there was such a thing as a civic-owned building for housing criminals, Scottish lairds punished offenders by placing them in iron yokes. The lairds would then exhibit the prisoners in public places. This yoke, or pillory for the head, was known as "the joug." A criminal being punished was, of course, "in the joug." Stone houses of detention came to be called "stone jougs," and in the course of time the spelling was modified to *jug.*

Coroner

IN old England the king had a personal representative, a "guardian of the pleas of the crown," in every county who looked after the ruler's interests. As early as 1194 there were numerous statutes under which a person who died without a will lost his property to the king. Consequently, the "coroner" (derived from "crown") investigated the death of every person in his district. By

1768 a *coroner* was designated to preside over the investigation of all violent and accidental deaths.

Subpoena

LATIN survived the fall of the Roman Empire by many centuries. Recent changes in Roman Catholic patterns of public worship seem likely to cause the classical language to retreat from its last major stronghold. As late as the fifteenth century Latin was the language of worship, scholarship, and law. Even though a witness to whom it was addressed couldn't read a word of Latin, the document commanding an appearance in court was written in that language.

A person required to appear as a witness and receive a penalty for failure to show up was served a paper that began, *Sub Poena ad testificandum.* In the case of a civil action in which a judge wanted documents produced, the summons read, *Sub poena duces tecum.* In common speech the classical term for "under penalty" was fused into a single word, *subpoena,* that designates a legal summons—even though it may be written entirely in English.

Cheat

UNDER medieval law a title to real estate could lapse in many ways. Property affected by such a lapse was called an "escheat" and became forfeit to the king. These cases were so numerous that some rulers employed escheators to look after their interests. Usually working on a commission basis, these fellows seized property at every opportunity. If they didn't violate laws, they certainly trifled with justice. Because of the questionable practices of these royal agents, it became customary to call any dishonest person a *cheat.*

Rigmarole

DURING early feudal times the official who made out tax lists was called a "ragman" and his list written on sheepskin was known as a "ragman roll." When Edward I of England invaded Scotland in 1296, he advanced leisurely, stopping in captured towns, forcing nobles and gentry to sign a ragman roll promising allegiance to their new king. After the subjection of Scotland was complete, Edward sent couriers to read the long lists in public places. Some of his messengers didn't take their task seriously, and they reeled off

the lists in such a hurry that the lists were difficult to understand. Thus the ragman roll eventually emerged into modern English as *rigmarole,* meaning any jumble of words.

Trial

AMONG the most vexatious problems for farmers in the Middle Ages was the separation of trash and impurities from the fruits of harvest. Grain was sifted and blown to remove chaff, while wool was handpicked to rid it of burrs and other impurities. From the colloquial Latin word *trier* ("to sort"), any act of separating good from bad was termed a "trial."

Courts borrowed the ancient farm word and applied it to the process of sifting evidence. After the jury system was established in courts of law, the importance of picking good evidence from bad became so great that the entire legal process came to be called a *trial.*

Rag

LIFE in "Merrie England" was far from merry for those out-side the privileged class. Many vagrants and drifters fared worse than today's street people. Those responsible for running undesirables out of town often set dogs upon their victims. Many of these vagrants had to run for their lives. The dogs would tear their clothes to shreds, literally reducing them to rags. As a result, those who cheered on the dogs were said to rag their quarry. The expression has now lightened somewhat, with *rag* meaning a ver-bal attack ranging from banter to taunt.

Alcatraz

PROBABLY the best known prison in America, Alcatraz owes its name to a chain of circumstances stretching back to the conquest of Spain by the Moors in the eighth century. The new rulers were intrigued by a strange bird frequently seen there. Mistakenly regard-ing its huge pouch as a container for water, they called the bird the *al catraz*—from the Arabic name for a bucket on a water wheel.

Seamen picked up the colorful term and applied it to large birds that fly over oceans. Finding great numbers of these birds on a tiny island in San Francisco Bay, explorers called the huge rock "Alcatrarsa." Named after the bird we know as the pelican, Alcatraz was long renowned for its ability to clip the wings of tough "birds" and keep them permanently grounded.

Beat the Rap

COURTROOM procedures change more slowly than many other customs. One of them, the formal rapping of a gavel, has served for centuries to open and close legal sessions. In the nine-teenth century, so long as testimony was being heard or delibera-tions were in progress, the accused had a chance. Even the pronouncement of sentence did not close the case; the situation was not hopeless until the judge rapped on his desk. Defense attorneys used every possible means to *beat the rap* or to prevent their clients from being sentenced. Consequently, the expression now stands for any method of avoiding a penalty.

Jury of Twelve

TRIAL by jury is not a modern institution. In ancient Greece men accused of crimes were tried by fellow citizens who were selected by lot. There was no standard number of jurors. Several city-states used as many as 570, and in some instances every citizen had the right to vote for or against an accused man.

During the Middle Ages the jury system died out. It was revived in England around the fourteenth century when institutional religion was at the height of its power. When a question arose as to the proper number of jurymen, church leaders specified twelve. They pointed out that Solomon had twelve officers. There were twelve tribes of Israel, and Jesus had twelve disciples. Use of this sacred number was felt to guarantee that the Holy Spirit would guide decisions and lead juries to proper verdicts. Hence English law came to specify that a trial jury should include neither more nor less than twelve "good men and true."

Kangaroo Court

WHEN the English explorer Capt. James Cook returned from Australia in 1771, he was branded a liar. People disbelieved his reports of a strange animal that hopped about on two legs and stood as high as a man, which he reported the natives called a "kangaroo." Many who heard his accounts doubted their truth, and there was great joking about kangaroos.

When a few specimens were brought to Europe, they created a sensation. Anything marvelous or unusual was likely to be termed "kangaroo." For example, an 1835 issue of the *Gentleman's Magazine* described an eccentric horseman as holding his reins with "kangaroo attitude." Settlers in the New World used the word to stand for any type of irregular gathering. During Reconstruction following the Civil War, a "kangaroo convention" held in Virginia made national headlines.

Criminals who adopted the odd word applied it to a "court" held by inmates of prisons. In such a proceeding, old-timers charged newcomers with such offenses as breaking into jail or being lousy and trying to scratch. Influenced by the prominence of irregular political gatherings, any extra-legal sham hearing came to be known as a *kangaroo court*.

Posse

NOVELS and movies about the American West have made *posse* a household word. However, it had won a respectable place in the vocabulary of crime and punishment much earlier.

No peace officers of modern times even approach the authority of a medieval English sheriff. He was vested by the crown with power to repress riots and other disturbances, no matter what their nature or extent. In a time of emergency this officer could employ the full power of his county—designated as *posse comitatus* in legal documents of the era. Such a body consisted of every able-bodied man above the age of fifteen except clergy and noblemen. Riding at the head of this motley and disorganized body, a sheriff often acted in high-handed fashion. Yet as late as 1765, when Blackstone began his famous commentary on the law, the English posse remained a standard instrument of law enforcement.

Settlers in America applied the name of the sheriff's legal band to all self-constituted bodies of citizens who took the law into their own hands.

Burglar

THE Middle Ages were a dark and troubled time. People were defensive much like people in cities are today. Instead of security alarms, the castles of the Middle Ages were fortified with moats and iron bars. From the Latin word *burgus* ("fortified place") came the term "burglar" as a title for a person who broke into a castle or church in order to steal. The importance of this special type of crime is indicated by a document issued in 1268. In it the three most common types of lawbreakers are listed as "murdritores and robbatores and burglatores."

Later British statutes made several refinements in the definition of a burglar. In 1916 it was stipulated that the name be reserved for one who breaks into a dwelling between 9:00 P.M. and 6:00 A.M. with the intention of committing a felony. If convicted under these limitations, the burglar received an automatic life sentence.

American courts have discarded limited definitions and fixed sentences. Any person found guilty of breaking and entering a dwelling or public building is termed a *burglar,* and the sentence given to such a law breaker may vary from very light to extremely severe.

Blackmail

THOUGH "blackmail" has come to stand for illegal extortion, it originated among respectable farmers of Scotland. As late as the sixteenth century, most of their farmland was owned by English noblemen. These absentee landlords charged very high rent. From the ancient Scottish term for tribute, such rent was called "mail." Rental agreements always stipulated that payment be made in silver or white mail.

Farmers who had no cash were sometimes permitted to pay in produce or black mail. Since prices fluctuated widely, greedy landlords often took advantage of penniless tenants and squeezed out black mail worth a great deal more than the cash amount of the rent.

People who extort hush money from a guilty party are as merciless as the landlords were in dealing with their tenants. B*lackmail* came to mean a bribe paid a person holding an advantage over another.

Jailbird

FOR centuries European law made some crimes punishable by public exhibition in a humiliating position. In England such offenses were usually the occasion for using the stocks. But on the Continent it was customary to place female prisoners in large iron cages suspended a few feet from the ground. Since the felon in such a predicament strongly resembled a bird in a cage, it became common to speak of her as a "jailbird." The word caught the imagination of the public, and *jailbird* came to be applied to any criminal behind bars.

Lean Over Backward

AS late as the eighteenth century, legal scales were weighted against accused persons. English judges of the period gained a reputation for an especially high-handed administration of justice. Many of these officials owed their appointments to political influence and were notorious for "leaning," or showing open prejudice in favor of the prosecution. This was especially true in cases of treason because condemned traitors forfeited all their property to the crown.

Vigorous cleanup campaigns led to a period of careful appointments, and many new justices were alert to the civil rights of accused persons. To avoid any suggestion of leaning toward the crown, some of them went to opposite extremes. Such an overly conscientious judge was said to *lean over backward*, and the phrase came to stand for any stickler who went beyond the call of duty.

Villain

LONG ago, the word "villain" was used to describe serfs in feudal England. The word derived from the Latin word *villanus*, or one who lived on a villa (country estate). Unfortunately, poor, low-born rustic persons sometimes had little to lose by breaking the law, and the entire class came to be labeled as would-be law-breakers. The next step was to call all criminals, knaves, and scoundrels *villains*, no matter whether they lived in the city or on a farm. Nevertheless, as late as the sixteenth century, a peasant farmer was still called a *villain*, no matter how harmless he was.

CHAPTER 4

FINE ARTS AND RELIGION

RELUCTANT

STUMBLING BLOCK

PILGRIMS

PROFANITY

RAISE CAIN

ELEVENTH HOUR

HYPOCRITE

MINIATURE

TONE DOWN

CHOIR

HENCHMAN

CHRISTENING

STEAL THUNDER

HIGHLIGHT

RHAPSODY

MUSICAL NOTES

EASEL

PARSON

ANGEL

APOCALYPTIC

AWFUL

BALL

BEGGAR

CREED

GOOD-BYE

JUBILEE

PATTER

RANT

RENEGADE

SEMINARY

SOLEMN

THORN IN THE FLESH

TO A *T*

WASH ONE'S HANDS

GLOSS OVER

Reluctant

FEW poets have had so great an impact upon Western thought as did John Milton. His *Paradise Lost,* published in 1667, is a major work in English literature. Milton ignored conventional practices in writing his epic. Contrary to established custom, his verses, like many of Shakespeare's, were blank or without rhyme. Whenever he could not find a common English word to meet his need, Milton manufactured one from a Greek or Latin base.

One such tailor-made term was *reluctant,* which was based on a Latin expression denoting the struggling of a wrestler or gladiator. For hundreds of years no one had employed the expression. Milton borrowed it from classical literature, modified the forgotten sports word, and applied it to personal struggle. Other poets picked it up, and from their pages the word made its way into everyday speech.

Stumbling Block

IN 1534, when William Tyndale was was making one of the earliest translations of the Bible into English, he had difficulty with Romans 14:13. Paul wrote that Christians should not put a *skandalon* in another's path to cause them to fall from grace. The Greek word referred to "a spring of a trap," an unfamiliar item to the English. Tyndale therefore converted the old hunting term into a reference that fitted the experience of his time, coining the term *stumbling block* from having seen people trip over debris scattered in alleys. Later translators of the King James Version used the phrase, and the expression was absorbed into the language as any obstacle or source of error.

Pilgrims

INTERNATIONAL travel flourished in the Roman Empire. In many large cities it was not unusual to see a merchant or soldier who wore odd clothes and spoke a queer brand of Latin. Such a foreigner came to be called *peregrinus*, or "stranger." Although its meaning changed less than its spelling, the ancient term entered the English language as *pilgrim*. The New World settlers whom we revere as the Pilgrims were "strangers for conscience' sake."

Profanity

IN classical temples the area in front—*pro* (before) and *faunum* (temple)—was not considered a sacred place. Thus, by extension, anything "profane" could be treated without reverence.

Over a millennium later John Wycliff was struggling with the task of translating the Scriptures into fourteenth-century English. When he came to Ezekiel 23:38, he groped for a vivid way to express the idea of treating the sacred with contempt. What could be better than to render this as a "profane" action?

The word thus entered the language. Careless and irreverent speech of the era included the use of holy names as expletives. Such contemptuous treatment of sacred titles constituted abuse of the holy and came to be known as *profanity*.

Raise Cain

NO other volume compares with the King James Version of the Bible in its influence upon speech. Its impact was especially great in the late eighteenth century when religious leaders turned to Scripture for rules to govern every area of life.

Most parents of the era were strict with their children, yet a lax or indifferent father would let his youngsters run wild. Neighbors usually took it upon themselves to give a bit of advice in such cases. After making a pointed reference to the biblical story of the first murderer, the adviser would declare that Adam and Eve were largely responsible. After all, they reared the boy who became the killer of his brother Abel.

According to this reasoning any careless parent was likely to raise another Cain. Since the killer's name was synonymous with trouble and grief, a person who creates a disturbance by actions ranging from rearing an unruly child to making a disturbance is said to *raise Cain.*

Eleventh Hour

BABYLONIAN scholars developed one of the world's earliest systems of arithmetic. Since the system was based upon twelve, their common measurements were divided into a dozen parts. Such was the case with the day. Greeks took over many Babylonian ideas and developed sundials marking twelve hours of daylight.

Judea adopted such a system of time, and it was in use during Jesus' life. Hours were counted from daylight to dusk, with the twelfth hour marking the day's end. So in the parable of the laborers (Matthew 20:1-16) Jesus expressed the idea of lateness by saying that some came at the eleventh hour of sunlight.

Westerners later modified ways of counting time, making twelve o'clock mark both noon and midnight. Hence the sun is hardly halfway across the heavens at eleven. Nevertheless, the force of the New Testament story is such that, in spite of the sun's position, the *eleventh hour* symbolizes the latest possible time for action or decision.

Hypocrite

WESTERN drama stems from that of the ancient Greeks whose term for actor was *hypokrites*, which was derived from the verb "to pretend." An actor pretended to be someone else. The word eventually came to mean a pretender or liar and, as such, passed through Latin and Old French into English.

In the fourteenth century, while making the first English translation of the Bible, John Wycliffe had to indicate the idea in Matthew 23:10 of "playing the part of piety." He borrowed from the Greek and called the spiritual pretender a *hypocrite.* In spite of its earlier use in secular senses, the word was quickly linked with piety. Other shades of meaning disappeared, and *hypocrite* became the standard label for one who assumes virtue like an actor who hides his true self in a stage role.

Miniature

THE word "miniature" has no relation to "minimum," meaning "small." Instead, it is derived from *minium*, the Latin word for red lead or vermilion.

During the long centuries when monks hand-copied all books, they often elaborately decorated the initial letter on a page. These illuminated manuscripts make much use of vermilion.

These pieces of art made with *minium* were necessarily small. Because of this association, any small-scale adornment or representation came to be called a *miniature,* regardless of whether or not the famous pigment was used in the work.

Tone Down

DURING the last quarter of the eighteenth century, a group of rebels defied the conventions of art. Led by J. M. W. Turner, a group of English painters began using a wide variety of vivid colors. Inevitably, a reaction followed, and early nineteenth-century artists returned to the use of more subdued tones.

As the trend vanished, the owner of a bright canvas often covered it with a coat of oil or varnish in order to soften its tones. Many second-rate paintings, and a few fine ones, were treated in this fashion. Hence to *tone down* became a standard term indicating any move toward moderation or reduction of extremes.

Choir

AS a distinct dramatic form, tragedy came into being in Greece during the fifth century B.C. Greek tragedies consisted of a series of dramatic episodes performed by never more than three actors on stage at one time. A *chorus* commented on and advanced the plot by dancing and chanting odes to musical accompaniment. Roman theater also made use of the *chorus*.

Passing through Old French, the Latin term entered English as "choir." By the thirteenth century many cathedrals had elaborate choirs. Singers were usually divided into two groups, one of which sat on the north and the other on the south side of the chancel. They sang in antiphonal fashion and were not accompanied by instruments.

A modern *choir* is any organized company of singers or part of a church used by singers.

Henchman

ANGLO-SAXON terms for a stallion and for a groom or attendant upon riders were combined into "henchman." Long a title of distinction it was reserved for youths of rank who served at court or upon the staff of some medieval earl.

The office of henchman gradually fell into disuse, and when Queen Elizabeth formally dissolved the ancient corps of royal henchmen in 1565, leading noblemen followed suit. As a result, the name gradually dropped from speech.

Sir Walter Scott happened to discover the old word two centuries later. He felt it was picturesque enough to make a good designation for the chief gillie, or right-hand man, of a Highland chief. So he used the term in both *The Lady of the Lake* and some of the Waverly novels.

Reentering popular speech through the influence of Scott, the word crossed the Atlantic and became linked with the chief lieutenant of a political boss. Activities of many an unscrupulous American *henchman* caused the once-honorable title to be applied to any mercenary or venal follower.

Christening

CHRISTIAN missionaries visited Britain very early in the present era, winning converts among both the native Britons and the occupying Roman army. During the period when the savage Anglo-Saxons were overrunning the island, the flame of faith flickered many times but never quite died.

Among the legacies from Roman occupation was the verb "to christen"—used to signify the act of winning a convert. As early as A.D. 890, Anglo-Saxon documents mentioned the desire of churchmen to christen, or convert, those unreached by "the good news of Christ." It was customary to administer the rite of baptism as an outward symbol indicating that one had been christened. By 1250 "baptize" and "christen" were being used interchangeably. Converts adopted new names that were announced during the baptismal ceremony. Hence the new name was variously known as the given name, baptismal name, or christened name.

In the late Middle Ages, perhaps a century before the time of Columbus, common folk of England adopted the practice of using both a given and a family name. As baptism became the rule rather than the exception, ceremonies made the giving of a name more and more important, and the spiritual symbolism has lost some significance in the *christening* of a child.

Steal Thunder

FOR more than two centuries the English-speaking world has used the expression "stealing thunder" to mean the appropriation of any effective device or plan that was originated by someone else.

An obscure English dramatist was father of the phrase. For the production of a play, John Dennis invented a new and more effective way of simulating thunder onstage. His play soon folded, but shortly afterward he discovered his thunder machine in use for a performance of *Macbeth* at the same theater. Dennis was furious. "See how the rascals use me!" he cried. "They will not let my play run, and yet they *steal my thunder!*"

Highlight

LATE Renaissance painters experimented with many techniques, one of them being the emphasis of lights and shadows. It became standard practice to treat one's canvas as lighted up and was generally agreed that the focal point of the painting should be the area of greatest brightness. For example, in a portrait the forehead or cheek of the subject was likely to be the point of greatest light intensity.

These focal points of light became known in photography also. By the twentieth century, the expression *highlight* was borrowed from the world of fine art to signify the outstanding feature of any situation or occurrence.

Rhapsody

GREEK poets compared literary creativity with the art of a seamstress, for both engage in putting pieces together. From their terms for "song" and "stitch" these poets created a name for a song or poem stitched together. Passing into Latin *rhapsodia* came to be the standard designation for works such as Homer's *Iliad* and *Odyssey*.

Centuries later, wandering minstrels entertained crowds by reciting snatches of such rhapsodic works. Between selections from these immortal poems, the minstrels often told humorous stories or repeated popular fables. These vignettes that were disconnected, improvised, yet usually impassioned came to be known as *rhapsodies*.

Musicians took over the much-traveled expression, which originated in ancient sewing circles, to describe such compositions as
George Gershwin's famous *Rhapsody in Blue*.

Musical Notes

MUSIC was cultivated as a fine art in classical times.
However, it lost some importance for centuries after the fall of the
Roman Empire. Alone among the institutions that survived the barbarian conquest, the church took a keen interest in music. Many
devotional poems were set to stately melodies using the six notes
of the musical scale of antiquity.

One of the most widely used of these religious songs was a
hymn for Saint John the Baptist's Day. In its most popular arrange-
ment, the initial syllables of a six-line stanza were sung on an
ascending scale:

Ut quant. lapis
*Re*sinate fibril,
*Ma*ra Geastrum
*Fe*male quorum,
*So*lve pollute
*La*bia rectum,
*Sa*ncta Aenaeus.

Association of the initial syllables with the six-note musical
scale led the notes to take their names from the sounds. Later
musicians added one new note and changed "ut" to "do." Still,
the ancient hymn is commemorated in "re," "mi," "fa," "so,"
and "la."

Easel

DESPITE the popularity of early Italian Renaissance painters,
comparatively little is known about their working methods. For
example, there is no certainty that any particular device for holding the canvas was standard.

Matters changed in the seventeenth century when the Dutch masters came to the forefront. More methodical than some earlier artists, they insisted they worked best when their canvases were laid upon three-legged frames of special construction.

Such a frame bore some resemblance to the donkey, which was the chief beast of burden used by the Dutch. Consequently, painters transferred their name for the animal to their patient burden-bearing device. Adopted by English artists, the "little donkey" that holds a canvas came to be spelled *easel*.

Parson

CHURCHMEN of the early Middle Ages took most of their titles from Latin. One such term, *persona*, was applied to the rector of a parish, who often lived outside his area of responsibility. Such a man received the income from his appointment but often paid a vicar to substitute for him in his duties.

Though the persona was a "personage," or official of no little distinction, his title was quickly modified in popular speech. By A.D. 1250, it had taken form as *parson*. Long reserved for Roman Catholic dignitaries, the term eventually came to be applied to any evangelical clergyman or preacher.

Angel

ENLIGHTENED leaders of the ancient Hebrews were sometimes chosen to receive special messages from God. In describing how such revelations came to them, they could only say that Jehovah sent word by a messenger (*mal'ak*). In time this title came to be reserved to designate a divine envoy.

Scholars who later translated the Old Testament into Greek searched for an equivalent of the technical Hebrew term. They could find no exact substitute, so they employed *angelos,* a general designation for a messenger of any sort.

Missionaries carried the Christian message and vocabulary to

Teutonic barbarians in very early times. They, in turn, made major contributions to the speech and life of Britain's people. As early as the famous Lindisfarne Gospels, which were issued in Anglo-Saxon prior to A.D. 950, translators used "engel" in such passages as Matthew 22:30. Under the influence of French-speaking Normans who later conquered the island, the initial *a* was restored to the old biblical term and the word emerged into today's speech as *angel*.

Apocalyptic

ANCIENT Greek housewives employed special cloths to keep dust out of food pots. They even devised a technical word meaning "to take away the cover." Romans who borrowed the term from these housewives modified it to *apocalypsis*.

By 200 B.C. Judea was in a state of ferment that lasted for three centuries. National and international distress helped produce a stream of literature making predictions about the future. Hope of sharing in the future glory of God's kingdom made it somewhat easier to bear the burdens of the age. Since a document of this type helped "take away the cover" from the future, Jews called it an "apocalypse."

Though many apocalypses were produced, only one stood the test of time: the stirring and poetic account of John's visions on the island of Patmos. Today it is referred to as "The Revelation of Saint John," but to the early church it was known as "The Apocalypse." The impact of this dynamic document was so great that any vision or prophecy dealing with the coming of God's earthly reign is termed *apocalyptic* literature.

Awful

ATTEMPTS to enter the presence of God nearly always produce strong emotional effects. One of the most powerful of these effects is the worshiper's sense of his own inadequacy, made vivid by contrast with the infinite might of God. It was therefore natural for ancient Hebrew prophets to record their breathless dread in the presence of Jehovah.

Ninth-century translators, seeking to render the Bible into the common tongue of Britain's inhabitants, had difficulty with the concept of holy fear. They employed an Anglo-Saxon word for distress, but readers found it inadequate to convey the biblical idea. Later translators, therefore, devised a new term. In order to express the fact that God fills people with reverent awe, translators who worked early in the eleventh century used such phrases as "God . . . mighty and awefull" (Deuteronomy 10:17).

Pushed into English speech through the impact of Scripture, the vivid term slowly degenerated and was applied to any situation or person causing awe. The spelling was slightly modified, and by 1800 it had come to be used to indicate "great" or "exceedingly." Hence, the once-powerful term for reverence is now used in such phrases as "an awful mistake," and "awful case of flu," and even "an awfully long day at school."

Ball

THOUGH the Feast of Fools was observed elsewhere at different times, the pious folk of Naples insisted that it should come just before Holy Week. As a part of the ceremony in the cathedral, all the choirboys danced solemnly around the dean. They sang hymns as each took his turn catching a ball that was thrown by the dignitary.

Formal dancing parties later came to be popular in the same region. So noted was the ball dance in the house of worship that any elaborate dancing party came to be known as a *ball*.

Beggar

MEDIEVAL piety, carried to the extent of giving away one's goods and living in poverty, probably gave rise to the word "beggar." Lambert la Begue, a priest of the twelfth century in Liege,

Belgium, was greatly moved by the suffering resulting from the Crusades. He devoted much of his life to establishing a cloister for widows and orphans of those who had died fighting for the Holy Land. His name, modified by the influence of the Old Flemish *beghen* ("to pray"), gave title to zealous Beghards of the era—laymen who took no vows. They lived in cloisters and put all their money into a common purse which was used for relief of the poor. The Beghards were influential for more than two centuries, and at one time claimed two hundred establishments in Belgium alone.

Beghards were never mendicants, but their food and clothing was little or no better than that of derelicts who depended upon alms for their support. Therefore, the name of those who "made themselves poor for the sake of Christ" was modified and became attached to every type of indigent *beggar* of late medieval and modern times.

Creed

AT least as early as the first century, churchmen recognized the need for some way to test the sincerity and conviction of converts. One of the simplest ways was the use of a statement of faith, to which one had to subscribe in order to be admitted to the Christian fellowship.

Doctrinal formulas became more significant during the third century. Various heresies flourished, and the church was rocked by controversy. It became necessary for legislative bodies to give formal recognition to brief statements summarizing the official position of the church. One such statement was so old that it had long been attributed to the Apostles themselves; another was drawn up in A.D. 325 by the Council of Nicea. Both of these official formulas were written in Latin, and both began with the word *credo* ("I believe"). It was not long before that word was being used as the title, and the term entered English as *creed*.

In most early uses the word stands for the Apostles' Creed. By the time of Shakespeare, however, it was being used as a common noun, and any definite formula of belief—religious or secular—came to be known as a *creed*.

Good-bye

OUR universally used word of farewell, *good-bye*, is a monument to ancient piety.

For centuries, when people parted company, they said to one another, "May God be with you." By the time of Shakespeare the sentence had been shortened to "God buy you." Later ages abbreviated it still more, with the result that "good-bye" came into general use.

Jubilee

THOUGH the word *jubilee* is loosely used to mean any occasion of great joy, it properly refers to any fiftieth-anniversary celebration. One of the most famous of these celebrations was the great Jubilee Year in honor of Queen Victoria's half-century reign.

The word goes back to an ancient custom of the Hebrews. They set aside each fiftieth year as a season of celebration and change. In that year lands that had been sold were restored to their original owners or their heirs. Slaves were freed, and everybody took a rest. Not even the fields were cultivated.

The year was introduced by the blowing of a special trumpet in the temple. Such a trumpet was made of a ram's horn, or *jobel*, and the name became attached to the celebration. Passing through a number of languages, it entered English as *jubilee*.

Patter

THE quick-running patter of comedians doesn't conjure thoughts of the prayer habits of medieval monks. Yet the expression arose because of the slovenly way in which some medieval friars were accustomed to hurry through their devotions.

Then, as now, the most frequently used of all petitions was the Lord's Prayer. Said in Latin, it was commonly called the Pater Noster (from the opening words, meaning "Our Father"). So widespread was the practice of hurriedly mumbling the Pater Noster that the name, shortened to *patter*, came to stand for all rapid, glib talk.

Rant

ENGLAND experienced a great deal of trouble during the first half of the seventeenth century. The famous Gunpowder Plot in 1605 warned of growing tensions in the government. Sir Walter Raleigh was executed, and the Duke of Buckingham was assassinated, after which civil war broke out in 1642. After a decade of bitter fighting, Oliver Cromwell overthrew the throne and established the Commonwealth.

Religious differences were almost as great as political ones. Fanatical sects, often violently opposed to one another, competed for popular support. Among these groups was a party of extreme radicals who withdrew from the Seeker movement. They embraced pantheistic doctrines and held public meetings of the evangelistic type. Preachers of this persuasion pitched, snorted, and raved. As English seamen had recently borrowed a vivid Dutch term for "talking foolishly," it seemed appropriate to call these loud fellows "ranters."

Although the movement dissipated in less than a century, it made a lasting impact upon everyday speech. From this time forth any loud and incoherent speaker, whether behind a pulpit, mounted on a soapbox, or standing flat on the pavement, has been said to *rant*.

Renegade

DURING the Crusades an occasional Christian deserted and joined the Muslim army. Some of these men were greedy for reward while others were fugitives from European justice. In order to be fully accepted by their one-time opponents, such fellows usually adopted the faith of Islam. From a Latin term meaning "to deny," Spanish churchmen framed *renegado* as a label for the man who denounced his faith.

English borrowed the vivid title and modified it to "renegade." For three or more centuries the term was commonly used to designate the occasional turncoat who denied his religion for profit. At the same time it was applied to a deserter of any type.

The term of contempt was on the verge of dying out when it was revived by novelists who wanted a suitably vigorous name for a white man who deserted to the Indians during frontier warfare. Made prominent by western stories and movies, the term *renegade* has entered half the major tongues of the world.

Seminary

THE Latin term *seminarium*, meaning a "seed plot," was adopted into English with little change in meaning; however, it had a variety of spellings for four hundred years. A typical quotation, dating from 1658, advises a gardener that he should take "your grafted trees out of the seminary, and transplant them into the nursery."

Roman Catholics adapted the ancient term by the sixteenth century and used it to name a special kind of school in which young men were "planted" in order to be nourished for the priesthood. For a time, the fancy title for "a seedbed of scholars" achieved such popularity that it seemed likely to become the standard name for a school of any type. Seminaries for young ladies flourished in eighteenth-century America, then dropped into obscurity. Having swept all competitors from the field, *seminary* is now a standard name for a theological school for training priests, ministers, and rabbis.

Solemn

IT has been customary throughout the ages to observe certain days and seasons as especially holy. The Roman Catholic Church used the term *sollemnis* when referring to ceremonies performed in "all years." In time such a rite came to be clearly distinguished from local and occasional festivals.

Latin remained the language of scholarship and worship even when missionaries began winning converts. In Britain the word was used for an established or official ceremony, but eventually it was Anglicized to "solemn" and was applied to any practice linked with formal worship. Through frequent use *solemn* came to name anything of grave and serious nature.

Thorn in the Flesh

FEW sections of the world rival the Holy Land in number and variety of native prickly plants. At least two hundred species of shrubs and trees of the region are equipped with thorns. Some of them, like the acacia and the buckthorn, make travel difficult where they abound.

In New Testament times it was a common occurrence to brush against an armored plant. Sometimes a thorn broke off, leaving its point embedded in the flesh. Readers of the letters written by the apostle Paul had no difficulty in understanding his meaning when he described a source of personal vexation as *a thorn in the flesh* (II Corinthians 12:7).

Even in lands where thornbushes are not a nuisance to travelers, the phrase is used to describe any persistent problem.

To a *T*

ANCIENT Hebrew scribes did much of their writing with little brushes. Numerous letters were distinguished from one another only by patterns of minute brush marks. Because of their shape, these marks were commonly known as "horns." It became proverbial that a careful scribe copied material exactly—that is, "to a horn."

A reference to these little marks is included in the New Testament (Matthew 5:18). When John Wycliffe issued his famous English translation of the Bible in 1382, he referred to the "horn" as a "titil." This word was later spelled "tittle," and "to a tittle" became a proverbial expression for scrupulous care. Abbreviated in common usage, the phrase lives on. Now when something is done with precision, it is said to be done *to a* T.

Wash One's Hands

MODERN drama was born in the church where plays and interludes based upon the Bible were used for centuries as a means of instruction of illiterate parishioners. Strolling bands of minstrels also performed biblical dramas at street fairs and had a great impact upon popular thought and speech.

A favorite scene was the enactment of Jesus' trial before Pilate. There were few props to make the background seem realistic, but it was customary to bring in a basin of water. Pilate then washed his hands as he denied responsibility for the death sentence. This bit of stage play made a great hit with audiences. As a result to *wash one's hands* of a matter came into general use as an expression disclaiming accountability.

Gloss Over

RELIGIOUS, legal, and technical works have often included difficult words and phrases. Before printed books became abundant, it was customary to insert into a manuscript a gloss or explanation at each point where interpretation seemed difficult.

Many a gloss (from the Latin word meaning "explain" or "translate") actually clarified meaning, but some scholars who wrote between the lines or in the margin introduced meanings not consistent with the text. As a result, one who changed the meaning of a passage by means of marginal comments was said to gloss over it. Influenced by German, the term also acquired an additional meaning of giving a false interpretation or explanation. An early literary critic recorded his vexation at friends of a writer "who are tender of his fame and gloss over this foible by calling him an agreeable novelist." A modern sweetheart who has no notion of adding explanatory comments to a technical book may admit that he's prone to *gloss over* the faults of his lady love.

CHAPTER 5

DISCOVERY AND INVENTION

IRISH POTATO

GABARDINE

JUMBO

PICAYUNISH

PHAËTON

MOCCASIN

MAHOGANY

PINEAPPLE

COCONUT

SHANGHAI

RUBBER

FARFETCHED

MAP

WHISKERS

TORN BETWEEN TWO FIRES

OWN HOOK

PACIFIC OCEAN

CHOW

ARGENTINA

TATTOO

ALLIGATOR

CANNIBAL

RUN AMOK

BALSA

FOSSIL

SOY

WATER HAUL

BUCCANEER

COBRA

GO THROUGH
  CUSTOMS

TOBACCO

FAR CRY

Irish Potato

SPANISH explorers discovered white potatoes grown by the Incas high in the Andes Mountains of South America. They brought the vegetable home, but it found no favor in Europe. A few plants were cultivated in botanical gardens as curiosities; most people, however, refused to eat their tubers.

Then a succession of crop failures produced famine conditions in Ireland. Peasants were persuaded to try the strange vegetables from America, and within a few generations white potatoes were among the major food crops of the nation. Since the Irish were the chief users, the plant came to be known as the *Irish Potato*.

Gabardine

FEW movements in history have been more thrilling than the pilgrimages of the Middle Ages. Many people traveled to shrines throughout Europe and even to the Holy Land. Pilgrims continued to visit some of the shrines at enormous sacrifice of time and money. They wore an unofficial but characteristic garb: a gray cowl bearing a red cross and a broad-brimmed, stiff hat. Pilgrims carried a staff, a sack, and a gourd. They usually traveled in company with other adventurers, singing hymns as they walked and begging food from those they met.

Since a particular type of upper garment was worn by the pilgrim, it gradually came to be identified with the journey itself. A will filed in 1520 included this bequest, "Unto litill Thomas Beke my gawbardyne to make him a gowne." From the garment the term came to refer to the coarse material from which it was customarily made. Slight modifications in spelling produced *gabardine*—a kind of cloth that passed from the religious pilgrim's vocabulary into general use.

Jumbo

LATE in 1869 a hunting party captured one of the largest elephants ever seen in West Africa. The natives had a superstitious fear of the thirteen-thousand-pound beast, and in their dialect, they spoke of him as being possessed by a *jumbo*—or evil spirit. Traders who bought the elephant thought the native word to be his name and called the big fellow "Jumbo."

Jumbo was shipped to London and placed in its zoological garden. He attracted many visitors but would have made no contribution to modern speech had it not been for a master salesman, Phineas Taylor Barnum.

Seeking a special attraction for his new Barnum and Bailey Circus, the American turned to Jumbo. He bought the animal in February 1882 and began billing him as the star attraction in his new circus. Among Barnum's many publicity stunts, he persuaded Philadelphia merchants to offer a new shade of gray—alleged to match the elephant's hide—that briefly sold as "jumbo."

Barnum's showmanship made the name of the elephant a household word before the close of 1882. Borrowed by advertising copy writers with the capitalization dropped, *jumbo* entered common speech as a vivid synonym for "huge."

Picayunish

SPANISH adventurers who settled in Florida and Louisiana established their own currency system. Its smallest unit was the half real, worth about 6 ¼ cents and known to later Creoles as the "picayune."

Merchants and traders didn't like to deal with picayunes because many customers were prone to quibble over its exact value in merchandise. This annoyance led the name of the coin to be attached to anything of trifling value. Consequently a person who quibbles or finds fault over any petty matter is said to be *picayunish,* or as troublesome as a frugal housewife spending a picayune.

Phaëton

IN Greek mythology Phaëton was the son of the sun god Helios (Apollo) and a nymph who was not divine. Helios promised his son a wish, and Phaëton asked to drive the chariot of the sun for one day. A mortal, Phaëton could not control the fiery steeds. They flew so high the earth froze and so low rivers dried up. The inhabitants of earth called to Zeus for help. He hurled a thunderbolt at Phaëton, knocking him from the chariot to his death.

Phaëton's name was forgotten for centuries, but during the Renaissance Europeans rediscovered classical literature. During this time, there were many sports noted for daredevil driving, and consequently any dashing handler of the reins was nicknamed *Phaëton.*

Eventually the term for a reckless driver was attached to a light four-wheeled racing carriage. When automobiles were invented, it passed to a touring car. By 1906 phaëtons were being produced by Duryea, Packard, and Walters.

Moccasin

EARLY adventurers who explored North America were amazed to discover the quality of workmanship among some Indian tribes. They found the native craftsmen especially proficient in mak-

ing leather gear—for which there was an abundant supply of deerskin. Using soft doe hide, the Indians made a type of loose footwear that was well adapted for use in the forests. Among the Powhatans and Ojibways such a shoe was called a *mockasin.*

When John Smith reached Virginia in 1607, he wrote a description of "mockasins, or Indian shoes." Colonists found the odd footgear easy to make and long wearing. Lacking tools and European leathers, many pioneers adopted deerskin shoes. A New Hampshire proclamation of 1704 even required every householder to include "one pair of magasheens" as part payment toward a special tax.

Worn throughout the northern colonies, the name of the shoe was standardized as *moccasin* and became an important type in the boot-and-shoe trade.

Mahogany

FEW words in common use have so obscure an ancestry as "mahogany." Its origin is a puzzle. Students of language long believed it to be borrowed from the Carib Indians, but modern research showed "caoba" to be the Carib name for the tree.

There's a strong tradition that Sir Walter Raleigh found this fine wood in the West Indies and brought specimens back to England around 1595. He must have misunderstood some native whom he questioned about its name, for he described it as "mahogeney." Regardless of the way the name was found, it stuck.

Within a century English shippers were doing a brisk import business. When the Swedish scientist Linnaeus listed the exotic tree in his famous botanical index, he took the English name as standard. Furniture makers adopted *mahogany* as a major material, and the vagrant word entered world speech.

Pineapple

EARLY Europeans had only one fruit of any consequence — the apple. Because of its great importance, its name was widely used. It became customary to speak of the seed pod of any tree or shrub as its "apple." For example, the cone-shaped fruit of the pine tree was known as the pine-apple. Until the middle of the seventeenth century, any reference to a pine-apple was in that sense.

In 1655 the works of a celebrated Italian traveler reached England. Pietro della Valle had been to the New World, and unlike many travelers of the period, he made careful notes about plant and animal life. One of the fruits, he wrote, "resembles in shape our common Pine-Apple."

Other explorers noted the fruit's marked resemblance to the pine cone and followed Pietro's example in speaking of it. As a result the tropical delicacy, grown hundreds of miles from the nearest pine tree, came to be known as the *pineapple*.

Coconut

PORTUGUESE parents of the sixteenth century frequently threatened their children with a bogey man called "Coco," from a Latin expression for skull. No one had ever seen a coco, but any child could describe his grotesque face.

Traders who first penetrated the Pacific islands had a rude shock. On many islands they found a variety of palm tree which bore a large brown nut. Each nut was about the shape of a human head and bore three black marks that resembled two eyes and a mouth. It looked so much like a bogey that they called it the *coconut*.

Shanghai

DURING the era of the sailing vessels the ship's captain had absolute authority at sea. He was both judge and jury and could order the death penalty for any seaman who refused to obey him. Once a man went aboard ship and cleared the harbor, he was at the mercy of his commander.

The expansion of shipping created such an acute demand for seamen that press gangs grew up in many cities. They would ply a man with whiskey, then deliver him to a shorthanded ship's captain for a fee. Country boys who wandered into the city were slugged and hustled aboard ship while unconscious. These abuses flourished in European and American ports for many years. They were finally outlawed, only to spring up on the other side of the world.

Shanghai was the chief shipping center of the East; nearly every big vessel in oriental waters stopped there. Shipping agents began supplying the crew for any ship's master willing to pay the freight—the new sailor's first month's wages in advance. This trade proved so lucrative that gangs lost all scruples. They made a common practice of capturing seamen from one vessel, then selling them to masters of another. So notorious was the port that American seamen coined a new verb, *shanghai,* to describe any kidnapping.

Rubber

ON his second voyage to "East India," Columbus found natives playing with a substance they called *caoutchouc.* It would stretch and then snap back into shape; when made into balls it would bounce. Scientists who examined the odd substance agreed that it was unlike anything known in Europe, yet they confessed themselves unable to imagine any use for it.

Small quantities of caoutchouc were brought to Europe, but it remained a curiosity for more than two centuries. At length someone discovered by accident that the material could be used for removing the marks of a lead pencil. Hence, bookkeepers termed it "lead-eater."

Around 1780 Joseph Priestley experimented with a bit of caoutchouc, hoping to find some use more important than erasing the errors made in ledgers. He failed and decided that it would never be of value except for rubbing out pencil marks. Consequently, he called it "East India rubber." Soon the nickname of the one-job substance was abbreviated to *rubber.* Its name serves as a perpetual reminder that civilization was once at a loss as to what to do with a substance of a thousand uses.

Farfetched

IN some respects the fifteenth and sixteenth centuries were among the most colorful of modern times. This was the age of exploration and adventure. New continents were being discovered; strange people and incredible beasts were being found.

All sorts of exotic things were brought back to Europe by sailors and explorers. Odd yellow tubers, called potatoes, came from the West Indies. Parrots were imported from Africa and tobacco from Virginia. Because such curiosities were fetched from afar, they were termed "farfetched." In 1583 a London merchant slyly suggested to his customers that "far-fetched and dearly bought is good for ladies."

Adventurers brought home fantastic tales as well as strange objects. Some of them described an altogether unbelievable animal they called the kangaroo. Others told about land, people, and animals that have never existed, for this was the golden age of travel fiction. After being at sea a few months, a man could come home with a pack of fantastic lies and find someone gullible enough to swallow them. So many tales fetched from afar were proved false that any improbable report came to be labeled *farfetched,* or extremely unlikely.

Map

GREEK geographers of the sixth century B.C. developed considerable skill in making charts to guide sailors and travelers. Then the Romans extended the art by engraving scale representations of the Empire on fine marble slabs. These devices, and the more abundant clay tablets, proved extremely cumbersome, so someone thought of painting geographical charts upon cloth.

For this purpose the most suitable material proved to be fine table linen, or *mappa.* This led to the practice of calling any flat geographical chart a *map.*

Whiskers

EARLY in the development of commerce between Britain and Scandinavia, the Norsemen also exported a word used for any type of cluster or bundle. With its spelling modified to "whisk," the term was adopted as a name for material used in making small brushes and brooms. Such a tool, or whisker, became a standard piece of household equipment.

Centuries later, sailors reintroduced the custom of wearing long facial hair. The bristles on a man's chin were compared with fibers of a brush, and any crop grown on the face came to be known as *whiskers*.

Torn Between Two Fires

IN the age of chivalry any knight worthy of the name was expected to offer his life in defense of the honor of some fair lady. Such gallant displays helped to emphasize romantic love. When a knight gazed upon the purity and beauty of someone like Eleanor of Aquitaine, or when a maiden was guarded by a brave knight, their hearts were ignited with a "passionate flame." Many stout swordsmen were proud to confess themselves all but consumed by "the fyre of luv."

Some fellows were unable to choose between sweethearts. Their hearts blazed not with one fire but with two. Under the circumstances the smitten one would pluck his lute and sigh at his misfortune at being *torn between two fires*.

Own Hook

THE Grand Banks off the coast of Newfoundland have long been famous as the silver mines of the sea, where a man could pull up many scores of fine codfish in a day.

Sea captains who could afford to do so preferred to hire crews by the season. Many an adventurer signed on a fishing boat, however, as a semi-independent operator. He provided his own gear and in return for passage and food gave the master or owner part of his catch. Such a fisherman was described as sailing "on his own hook."

To keep count of his daily take, such a fellow cut out the tongue of each fish he caught and strung it on a wire. In poor seasons regular crew members fared better than the independents, but when cod were abundant, fat profits came to any man fortunate enough to be there as his own master. Soon it became customary to say that one who takes chances by operating in solitary fashion does so on his *own hook.*

Pacific Ocean

FERNÃO de Magalhães, a Portuguese navigator better known as Magellan, left Spain for the New World on September 20, 1519, commanding a fleet of five ships. The long, hard voyage seemed to be dogged by bad luck. Water supplies ran very low, and the ships' biscuits became infested with insects.

Geographers had long insisted that there must be a vast uncharted ocean west of South America. On the very day that men in Magellan's long boats discovered a passage, some of his crew members mutinied and fled back to Europe with the *San Antonio.* He insisted on going ahead, sailing westward. With a fresh breeze in their sails, his ships entered a bright and intensely hot region. Unlike the Atlantic, whose gales they had fought in order to reach the New World, this vast body of water was placid for day after day. As a result Magellan gave the newly discovered ocean a name that entered English as "Pacific."

Later it was found that the Pacific Ocean covers one-third of the earth's surface and has an area greater than that of all the land on the planet. Though it includes vast regions where winds and waves are comparatively subdued, other sections of the great ocean spawn the world's most fearful storms. The name had stuck before this discovery was made, however, so it seems likely that future generations will continue to call some of earth's most turbulent waters the *Pacific Ocean.*

Chow

ENGLISH-SPEAKING adventurers had a hard time establishing outposts in the Far East. They found it difficult to pronounce native words, so they adopted sing-song versions. That's how they remembered an ancient term for mixed pickles. Stumbling over the sonorous name from cities in China or India and unable to approximate the native sound, they called the dish *chow-chow*. No adventurer could tell what ingredients went into it, so its name attached to any dish whose components could not be distinguished.

For centuries, masters of sailing vessels drove their men mercilessly. There was fierce competition for cargo, and owners prided themselves on setting speed records. In 1850 the American clipper *Oriental* made the run from Hong Kong to London in just 97 days. On long voyages cooks often ran short of food and had to serve any kind of stew they could make. Sailors complained at having to eat such chow-chow but received it so often they cut the term in half and began using *chow* to stand for any food—mixed or pure.

Argentina

LLAMAS grazing on the slopes of Mount Potosi in 1545 pulled up a clump of shrubs by their roots. With eyes bulging, their native owner stared at a vein of solid silver laid bare by the animals. For a few months he managed to keep his secret hidden. Then the Spanish masters learned of it and took possession.

The wealth of the ore proved far greater than anyone could have imagined. Potosi became the largest town in Alto Peru (now Bolivia). Its population jumped to 160,000 as it became the chief city of the New World. Native miners were worked in merciless fashion. Four out of five died within a year of going underground, but they brought out white metal by the ton. Meanwhile prospectors had no success in the vast region drained by the Rio de la Plata (River of Silver). In spite of the name given by early optimists, the mines proved scarce and poor. The title stuck, however, and became attached to an entire province.

When the province became a nation in 1816, leaders decided to name it for the precious metal. Turning to Latin for "silver," they called their land *Argentina*. To this day, though, the Silver Republic has yielded only a fraction of the bullion that other South American nations with less colorful names had yielded.

Tattoo

ONE of the world's greatest explorers, the British navigator Capt. James Cook, commanded three voyages to the Pacific Ocean and sailed around the world twice. The first European to visit Hawaii and Australia's east coast, he led expeditions in his ship, the *Endeavour,* that resulted in the establishment of colonies throughout the Pacific region by several European nations.

Captain Cook's expedition of 1769 brought him another kind of fame by adding a colorful term to the English language. While spending six weeks in Tahiti, he was intrigued by a strange native custom in which the islanders made gashes in their skin and inserted black pigment. When the wounds healed, they had permanent body markings.

Stumbling over the Tahitian word for this operation, *tatau,* Captain Cook made diary notes about the practice of "tattowing." He was especially interested in the way natives bore the pain of the operation and in the fact that they decorated every part of the body. Today the word *tattoo* names any method of making permanent marks under the skin, though third millennium operators scorn knives and soot in favor of electric needles and special inks.

Alligator

SPANISH explorers in the New World were astonished to find a beast there that looked like a huge lizard, so they referred to it as *el lagarto*, the Spanish word for the beast. In 1568 its first recorded use in English appeared in *The Travailes of an Englishman*. The author, Job Hortop, wrote, "In this river we killed a monstrous

Lagarto or Crocodile." In 1614 Sir Walter Raleigh considered the creature to be of the same strain as those long familiar in Egypt. Scientists now recognize that the animal is neither an overgrown lizard nor a crocodile. Still, *alligator* preserves a hint of the awe with which the creature was regarded by those who first saw it in the rivers and swamps of Florida.

Cannibal

THE natives whom Columbus encountered in the Lesser Antilles on his second voyage to the New World in 1493 told him their name was "Canibalis." Actually, this was a colloquial expression for a part of the whole tribe of Caribs. Comparatively tall people with wavy hair, these Canibalis were good canoe makers and sailors who gave their name to the Caribbean Sea. Soon it was discovered that some of them practiced the eating of human flesh. Stories of their exploits created a great stir in Europe where the bloody practice was known only from ancient history. By 1719 when Daniel Defoe wrote *Robinson Crusoe*, the term had become standardized as *cannibal* and was applied to people-eaters everywhere.

Run Amok

DURING the Age Of Exploration, Europeans encountered many strange sights in faraway lands. They then returned home and wrote about their adventures for the amazement of others. A case in point is the Italian account of strange opium-induced actions in Indonesia, which was translated into English in 1519: "There are some of them [under the influence of opium] who…go out into the streets and kill as many people as they meet…these are called *Amuco*."

Impressed with the vivid scene, the English made use of it in the expression *run amok*, meaning in a frenzy to do violence or to be in a confused state.

Balsa

W HEN Spanish adventurers began to explore the Pacific coast of South America, they noticed that natives used rafts quite different from those on the Atlantic side of the continent. Lashed together with vines or crude ropes, the vessels were strangely buoyant and could be used even in very rough water. From a Spanish term for "fishing-float," Europeans termed the buoyant South American raft a "balsa." Applied to the vessel itself, this usage persisted as late as 1847 when William Hickling Prescott in his famous *History of the Conquest of Peru* wrote that invaders transported "the commander's baggage and the military stores on some of the Indian balsas."

From their introduction to the craft, Europeans recognized that these "fishing floats" gained their distinctive floating property from logs of a special tree, which they also called *balsa*.

Investigation showed balsa to be about half the weight of cork—then the lightest lumber in general use—and much stronger. A raft made of balsa is almost as versatile and sturdy as a boat. To support his theory that Polynesia must have been settled from America, Thor Heyerdahl built a large rigged balsa raft, the *Kon-Tiki*. With no source of power other than that from winds and ocean currents, he sailed from South America to a Polynesian island in a voyage of about three months.

Fossil

M EDIEVAL Europeans made extensive use of ditches, trenches, canals, and moats, naming them from a Latin expression meaning "to dig." Great numbers of these "fosses" drained, girdled, and protected cultivated fields.

Sometimes a farmer unearthed what seemed to be a bone or tooth. Queer objects of this sort accumulated in numbers sufficient to interest scientists. Against strong opposition it was finally shown that a *fossil,* or relic dug from a fosse, was the remains of an animal or plant that had flourished in prehistoric times. The name clings to all organic clues to the distant past—though most are now found through organized archeological searching rather than from being stumbled upon in ditch digging.

Soy

FEW centuries have matched the sixteenth in daring and discovery. The Portuguese found routes to India, Malacca, China, and even Japan. Unfortunately these lands proved something of a disappointment—unlike Mexico and Peru they had little precious metal. Early European traders, however, were pleased with one thing they did find—a novel seasoning for food. Unlike such familiar and valuable spices as nutmeg and cinnamon, the new Chinese delicacy was a liquid. Cooks who prepared it from salted native beans and oil called it *sho-yu*. Twist their tongues as they might, the traders couldn't make the right sounds. Mangling the Chinese words almost beyond recognition, they settled with the term *soy*—applied first to the sauce and much later to the bean from which it is made.

Water Haul

THE Normans who followed William the Conqueror introduced many new words into Britain. Among them was an Old French term for "to pull or draw." English seamen who adopted the term modified it to "haul" and used it in connection with pulling sails and nets.

Centuries later Yankee fishermen discovered many fine banks in the North Atlantic. Special vessels were designed for trawling—or dragging a big bag-shaped net below the surface of the water. It was not always possible to know whether or not fish had been caught, so the nets had to be hauled up at intervals to check. Many an old salt must have spat with disgust after hauling in a net, only to discover it empty. Frequent experiences with the *water haul* on fishing boats led Americans to apply the vivid name to any type of wasted effort.

Buccaneer

AMERICANS who fondly remember swashbuckling movies will be surprised to learn that the word "buccaneer" equates with "barbecuer."

The English borrowed the French word *boucanier*, which referred to a person on the Caribbean island of Hispaniola or Tortuga who hunted wild oxen or boars and then cooked them over a fire on a frame called a *boucan*.

Soon English, French, and Dutch boucaniers had a remunerative business intercepting Spanish galleons laden with gold which were plowing the seas home to Spain from the South American mines. The first recorded use in English of *buccaneer* in this sense was in 1690.

One of the most famous buccaneers was Henry Morgan, who was even knighted by the king of England for capturing and destroying the city of Panama, which belonged to England's enemy, Spain. However, by 1700 these buccaneers began attacking ships of all nations, and the British, French, and Dutch governments classified them as pirates who were outlaws.

A modern buccaneer is a ruthless speculator or adventurer in business or politics.

Cobra

MANY reptiles can enlarge their necks when angry, and this characteristic has been familiar to observers of nature for thousands of years. Still, spice traders of the sixteenth century were incredulous when they first saw big oriental reptiles in action.

Sometimes reaching a length of twelve feet, the creatures are unusually domestic. They make nests of dried leaves, and after laying eggs in them they stay around until the young are hatched. When disturbed while guarding its nest, one of the deadly reptiles will raise its ribs and push them forward. With its elastic skin stretched tightly over the wide bony framework, the creature almost looks as though its head were wrapped in a protective hood.

Small wonder that Portuguese adventurers called it "snake with a hood," or *cobra de capella*. Many wild yarns about the hooded reptile were circulated in Europe. As late as 1668 some English scientists believed it had a head on each end of its body. That myth vanished when specimens were captured and studied. Eight or ten species were eventually distinguished and use of the full descriptive title was abandoned in favor of an abbreviated one. Therefore, the name of the hooded killer entered modern times as *cobra*— which is neither more nor less than the old Portuguese term for a snake of any kind.

Go Through Customs

THE modern customs station derives its name from the Middle English word "custume"—equivalent to "costume" or habitual mode of dress. This label was used so frequently that it attached to any common practice or usage, whether involving clothing or not.

One such common practice was that of collecting rents, dues, and taxes. Feudal rulers were careful to see that no one failed to pay customary charges, hence any levy exacted as a matter of course came to be known as a custom. This usage prevailed during nineteenth century America when most major ports held customs houses.

European kings continued the ancient practice of exacting a charge as a condition for permitting merchants to pass through cities on trade routes. In order to collect customary passage fees, officers had to be employed. In order to function, they had to have regular stations. So by the time Columbus discovered America, the customhouse was a familiar European institution.

As international travel broadened, it was natural to have officers check the luggage of tourists as well as to assess taxes upon imported goods of merchants. In popular speech the old word for a habitual tax was slurred into plural form, with the result that it is now customary for persons who cross national boundaries to *go through customs*.

Tobacco

OCTOBER 10, 1492, brought an end to the complaints of Columbus's weary and disgruntled crew members. That day, deck hands fished from the waves a green branch with a blossom on it. Before evening they also found a reed and a staff that bore carvings clearly made by human hands. No doubt about it, they were close to land!

Strange animals, queer plants, and odd customs were encountered almost daily. True, there was no evidence of the huge gold nuggets that were supposed to be lying around in abundance. Neither did he find the spices that were a major inducement for the voyage. Other exotic things dulled the edge of his disappointment, however. In his journal Columbus recorded on November 6:

> "My messengers reported that after a march of about twelve miles they had discovered a village with about one thousand inhabitants. . .They encountered many men and women carrying some sort of cylinder in which sweetly smelling herbs were glowing. The people sucked the other end of the cylinder and, as it were, drank in the smoke. Natives said they called these cylinders 'tobaccoes.'"

Spanish adventurers confused the Carib word for the reed tubes with the dried leaves burned in bowls at the end of them, and *tobacco* entered world speech to designate the odd plant from the Americas.

Far Cry

IN medieval Scotland, petty kings were accustomed to publicizing their edicts by means of criers. These men went from place to place, shouting the terms of royal proclamations. Some announcements were local, applying to a single town or district. A courier entrusted with a message of that sort was said to be given a "near cry."

In time of war or other national emergency, a crier might have to ride for days to complete his tour of duty. Such a "far cry" involved distances greater than the average man's travels of a lifetime. Hence, *far cry* came to be used as a synonym for "remote."

CHAPTER 6

COMPARISONS

DUMBBELL

HIGHBROW

APPENDIX

BUGLE

CHAIR

CRYSTAL

DIAMOND

EROSION

FORMULA

GYMNASIUM

INFANTRY

INTOXICANT

LENS

POLITE

READ

RECIPE

SERENADE

Dumbbell

DURING the late Middle Ages, bell ringing was a highly regarded art. Men spent years learning to "ring the changes" on bells of great cathedrals. In its simplest standard form this exercise called for a precise pattern of 5,040 notes played on seven bells. Since learners practiced for hours at a time for days on end, their noise was a public nuisance.

An unknown craftsman devised an elaborate rope mechanism to be used by apprentice ringers. The ringers went through all the motions but pulled "dumb bells"—counter-balanced weights or noiseless bells—rather than real ones. A workout with these instruments gave one plenty of exercise. So when an early health faddist invented a wooden apparatus for taking exercise, he named it the *dumbbell*.

Highbrow

FRANCIS Joseph Gall, an eighteenth-century German physician, spent his life in study of the human brain and founded the "science" of phrenology. After examining the heads of thousands of people, chiefly criminals and mental patients, he concluded that those with big heads (high foreheads) are smarter than others.

Gall's theories received tremendous publicity, and throughout most of the nineteenth century he was regarded as a pioneer in a new field of learning. Then other scientists began to ridicule his conclusions. Careful tests proved that a person with a big forehead was not necessarily a genius, but by 1875 the expression *highbrow* had already entered the language. First used in a complimentary sense for an intellectual, the term gradually lost standing and more often was applied to pseudo-intellectuals. Nevertheless it spawned two other words. *Lowbrow* entered the language in 1906, and in the 1940s *Life* magazine popularized the term *middlebrow*.

Appendix

FROM the Latin verb *appendere* ("to hang upon") scholars and scientists of the late Middle Ages called any accessory or "hanging on" thing an "appendix." This usage still survives in the publishing trade as a name for an addition to a document or book.

Early anatomists were interested in the fact that many organs of the human body bear small prolongations. It was natural to use the label for "something that hangs" to name such a growth. Centuries later it was discovered that there is a pouchlike formation at the point where the large intestine is joined with the small intestine. This formation, the cecum, is often marked by a "hanging body" so large that it dwarfs every other appendix in an organism, so it came to be known as the *appendix*.

Bugle

MEASURED by almost any standard the most important domestic animal of the Romans was the ox, or *buculus*. A live buculus provided power, and a dead one was a major source of food, leather, and other essentials. The name of the surly beast passed from Latin into several European languages and designated a bullock, wild ox, or buffalo from India or Africa. By the time it became standardized in English, the spelling had changed to "bugle."

Horns of the bugle or wild ox were widely used as musical instruments and hunting signals. Around 1750, Hanoverian jager battalions noticed that a metal version of the bugle's horn used in signaling by masters of the hunt gave a particularly penetrating set of notes. Adopted by continental fighting men, the German Flugelhorn proved so efficient that English light infantry decided that they, too, would put the bugle to new uses. It was this instrument that sounded many of the signals in the battle made famous by Tennyson's "Charge of the Light Brigade."

Made of brass or copper and somewhat smaller than the trumpet, horns of this sort proved so efficient that special music was written for them. "Reveille" and other modern calls have changed very little during the last 150 years, and the bugle is still shaped so that it resembles the ox horn whose name it bears.

Chair

PIECES of furniture designed for use by a single person have come to be common and cheap only in modern times. During the Middle Ages such a sitting piece was costly and relatively rare. In gatherings of all sorts, ordinary folk sat on the floor or upon benches. Only persons of importance had their own moveable perches.

From the Greek word *kathedra*, any four-legged piece of furniture with a back and two arms was known in Latin as a *cathedra*. Such a piece was used by a king on state occasions, by a judge presiding over court, by a mayor holding town council, and by a bishop exercising his office. Because the piece of furniture was the symbol of office and authority, to speak *ex cathedra* ("from the chair") came to mean exercising one's power to speak and expecting obedience with no questions asked. Medieval cathedrals were built to house the seat (*cathedra*) of the bishop.

As medieval universities multiplied after the thirteenth century, the piece of furniture signifying rank and dignity was naturally more and more common in places of learning. Students customarily occupied benches, and only a professor could sit in a chair. So much sitting was done with so much pomp by so many learned doctors that most other roles of the chair dwindled in importance by comparison. A professorship is still known as a "chair" in spite of the fact that such a piece of furniture is supplied to each student in a modern classroom. Benefactors of colleges and universities often establish an "endowed chair," and a professor is likely to refer to himself as "occupying the chair of English." Reflecting on this situation more than a century ago Ralph Waldo Emerson needled the academic world by insisting that "many chairs are made beds of ease." No doubt he meant professorial chairs and not sitting pieces for students!

Crystal

GREEK naturalists were greatly interested in certain strange stones often picked up from the ground. Though harder than granite the gemlike pieces were as transparent as ice. It was logical to give such a stone the same name as ice—*krystallos*, meaning "frozen into a crust." For thousands of years it was generally believed that ice actually petrified into chunks of mineral when subjected to long-continued action of nature. The Latin version of the word was *crystallum*, and it was used as such by Saint Jerome in his Latin version of the Bible now called the Vulgate. Today we know that the mineral quartz is not ice, but in English we preserve the ancient name as *crystal*. Fine glassware is so clear and hard that it resembles nature's own crystals.

Diamond

CHANCE was probably responsible for man's discovery of hard metals. By the time the Greeks built their city states, their artisans were familiar with a metal they could not cut. From a phrase meaning "I cannot tame," the artisans called such a substance *adamas*, meaning "invincible," or "untamable."

Passing into Latin without change, the term was long applied to the hardest known substance, which varied from one place to another. The term attached first to various metals, then to carborundum, and next to the white sapphire. Among the precious objects the roman emperors accumulated were colorless gems, crystals formed almost entirely of carbon. These jewels proved to be the hardest naturally occurring substance found on earth. It was proper that such a stone should take the title "invincible." Through the centuries as French evolved from Latin and then was transported to England with the Norman Conquest, *adama* became our *diamond*, which as the advertisement says, "is forever."

Erosion

THOUGH the modern rat was probably unknown to them, Romans were continually troubled with hordes of mice. From their term *rodere* ("to gnaw") we get the name "rodent."

Alchemists of the Middle Ages were greatly interested in the biting action of chemicals. Comparing this with the gnawing of a rodent, the process of cutting into metal with acid came to be called "erosion."

Around 1825 geologists began to call attention to the fact that rivers and glaciers scar land somewhat as acids and salts cut into metals in the laboratory. Not until 1879, however, was there any general recognition that erosion has major effects upon agriculture. Interest in combating the gnawing action of water is, therefore, quite recent. Yet wide publicity has made the interest so prominent that *erosion* has entered half the major languages of the world.

Formula

ROMANS are famous for their precise, methodical ways. They performed most duties with great care and even wrote exact directions for religious and political ceremonies. Any pattern of words which was to be used without change they called *forma* ("form"). A short passage became *formula* ("little form").

Centuries later European scholars revived many long-lost expressions. Among them was the Latin designation for a form of words such as a creed or oath of allegiance. Every nation had its special formulas by which kings were invested with authority, soldiers addressed their superiors, and worshipers participated in religious rites.

Eventually the much-used term was applied to words used in a physician's list of medicines or a housewife's favorite recipe, which had to be followed as carefully as a formula for behavior at court. Spreading from such everyday use the word gradually attached to unvarying sets of directions like those employed in chemistry, physics, and other exact sciences. Traces of the commonplace origin still cling to it; however, both the little recipe and the mixture produced by following the careful instructions for preparing a baby's bottle have the ancient title of *formula*.

Gymnasium

BY nearly every standard the Greeks were the most enlightened people of ancient times. They even developed a program of physical education at public expense because they felt that physical training was essential. It was limited to males, and they trained and competed in the nude to maximize the freedom of movement.

So from *gymnos* ("naked") the building in which they worked out was called a *gymnasion*. The Romans adopted both the building and the training program. With the efficiency for which they are famous, the Romans built many a new gymnasion so that their young men might be trained for sports and war. Even the profligate emperor Nero took interest in the program and gave a great central gymnasion to the city of Rome.

After the fall of the empire, the concept of physical education was forgotten for hundreds of years. Then, around the sixteenth century English scholars rediscovered the classical word, and now *gymnasium* designates any building devoted to physical education.

Infantry

HORSES were of immense value to ancient armies. They gave great mobility to units for scouting and pursuing. Since there were never enough mounts for everyone, soldiers with greatest seniority were usually given the horses. This meant younger soldiers marched and fought on foot. They were younger and less experienced than the cavalrymen and were called *infans*, which is Latin for "boy" or "foot soldier." Adapted into English, as well as many European languages, any foot-bound soldier too inexperienced for cavalry is a part of the *infantry*.

Intoxicant

ALL'S fair in love and war," but military leaders have frequently scorned ignoble tactics. That was the case in the days of the Greek states when the generals of Athens and Sparta refused to use poisoned arrows. Nevertheless, the generals met enemies who did employ poison, which they called *toxikos*, because arrows smeared with the poison were shot from a bow, or *toxon*.

The Romans, who mastered Greece, borrowed many of the Greek words, including the one which stood for "poison from the bow." They modified its spelling to *toxicum*, and the word passed into the speech of the European tribes whom the Romans subdued. By the Middle Ages the term was applied to any poison.

In English "toxic" came to mean anything poisonous and the temporary "poisonous" effect of alcohol.

Lens

GREEK scientists knew that a water-filled glass sphere served to concentrate light rays. Not until the thirteenth century, however, was there any real progress in making such optical instruments as crude spectacles.

Later craftsmen developed skills in producing elaborate bits of glass that bulged outward on both sides in regular curves. This convex piece was shaped very much like a lentil seed or *lens*.

Though the pealike vegetable of medieval times has been considerably modified by centuries of selective breeding, its name clings to most light-bending devices of the Atomic Age.

Polite

CRAFTSMEN of the ancient world developed a high degree of skill in working gold and silver vessels. When a particularly fine piece was finished, the artisan would rub it until it became *politus* or "polished." The barbarians who overran the Roman Empire had little care for the niceties of life. It made no difference to them whether a vessel was *politus* or not, so the word dropped from use.

Around the end of the fourteenth century, English churchmen revived the practice of polishing ecclesiastical ware with great patience. Looking about for a term to describe a burnished piece, the churchmen borrowed the Latin word and modified it to *polite*. From the care paid to "polite" gold and silver vessels, the word soon came to be associated with elegance and refinement. By the middle of the eighteenth century, *polite* was being used to mean courtesy in general.

Read

HUMAN beings have always wanted to peer into the future. Even today, palmistry or fortune telling with cards and astrology still have many followers.

In planning affairs of state, the Greeks and Romans arrived at some of their decisions by studying the entrails of fowls slain according to precise ceremonial rites. Among early Teutonic peoples one of the most important methods to predict coming events involved bits of wood on which symbols had been written or scratched. Such tokens were placed in a bag or folded cloth and solemnly shaken out so that the priest or head of the family could study them and from their patterns reach decisions or offer counsel. Because of this practice Old English speech included the term *raedan*, to mean "counseling," "interpreting," and "predicting."

Our word *read* was modified only a trifle. It still preserves some of the ancient sense of mystery, for even though we use standardized symbols, two people who interpret the meaning of the little black marks on white paper often disagree as to the significance and meaning of what they see; so *to read* something still involves interpretation.

Recipe

SINCE Latin was the universal language of medieval scholars, physicians used it in writing directions for compounding medicines. Virtually every prescription listed the ingredients in precise order and began with the Latin verb *recipe,* meaning "take."

Care in measuring and blending the ingredients of a tasty dish is also essential. Therefore, when housewives began to master the art of reading and writing, they adopted the apothecary's custom and made written lists of ingredients and steps in cookery. Inevitably such a set of directions took the pharmaceutical name and became familiar as the household *recipe.*

Serenade

NO one knows what gallant Latin lover first thought of singing tender melodies to his sweetheart at eventide. By modern times the custom was already firmly established. However, rainy and stormy weather was unsuitable for this delightful occupation. A cavalier consequently hoped that a clear, calm sky—which in Italian was called *serenata*—would prevail when he wanted to sing a love song under his lady's window. In time the melodies themselves came to bear that name, and in English the word was modified to *serenade.*

CHAPTER 7

MILITARY

TOWERING AMBITION

POINT-BLANK

UNSTRUNG

GUN

GAT

CATARACT

CRUSADE

SHIBBOLETH

BRACELET

MEDAL

QUOTA

THYROID

BASSINET

BUDGET

FIRST RATE

DREADNOUGHT

Towering Ambition

A PASSIONATE yearning for success is frequently described as "towering ambition." This expression owes its place in the language to the medieval passion for falconry. Many types of killer hawks were bred in captivity, then trained to capture game birds. A falcon's ability as a hunter was partly measured by the speed with which he gained enough altitude to swoop down on his prey. Because watchtowers were the tallest buildings of the period, the hawk that flew high in the air was said to "tower."

Many falcons were haughty and cruel and had little affection for anyone, not even the trainer who fed them daily. Such a bird's high "towering" in search of prey was not unlike the upward sweep of an ambitious person. So a man dominated by desire for success was said to "tower." With the decline of falconry the term was modified in popular speech, so that *towering ambition* came to stand for any ambition that is a controlling force in life.

Point-Blank

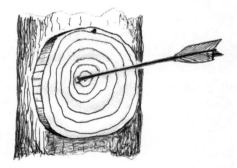

A NGLO-SAXON bowmen were among the first to develop a standard type of archery range. They used a flat target whose center was probably marked by a cross section of a tree limb, sawed into a disk and pegged in position. This white bull's-eye contrasted sharply with the body of the target and was the goal of expert marksmen. Eventually the blank spot was standardized at about the size of a crown piece. Even with the famous longbow, introduced by the Normans who conquered the island kingdom, it was difficult to hit the bulls-eye at any distance. Yet every boy with his first bow knew that in order to hit the target at all, he had to try for the blank.

It became customary to speak of close-range shooting as point-blank fire, and with the advent of firearms the term was attached to the use of the new weapons. *Point-blank* came to signify the limit of distance through which a trajectory remains approximately straight. Because such firing in gunnery is destructive, by extension the word came to mean "blunt" or "brutal" as in the expression "point-blank accusation."

Unstrung

IF the entire history of mankind is taken into account, the bow is probably the most important weapon ever invented. Guns have won and defended empires for only a few hundred years; the bow dominated military life for many millennia.

Despite its ancient lineage this weapon didn't reach its greatest development until modern times. English archers discovered that seasoned yew could be made into bows that stood as high as a man. Drawn back by a sturdy yeoman, an arrow from such a longbow would penetrate an inch of oak at a distance of a hundred yards.

One major difficulty was experienced with these formidable weapons. If kept constantly under tension, the bow soon lost its resilience. When it was not in use, it was desirable to slip one end of the bowstring loose. That placed its owner at a tremendous disadvantage if he happened to encounter an enemy who had his weapon poised.

Only the bravest of the brave could refrain from quaking when caught "unstrung" in this fashion. Surviving in colloquial talk for many generations, *unstrung* emerged into standard speech in the sixteenth century. It survives in the third millennium as an apt phrase to describe a state of great nervousness or fear.

Gun

LONG before the invention of gunpowder military men used crude catapults that threw great stones to batter down the walls surrounding enemy fortresses and cities.

Then as now, artillerymen were in the habit of giving names to their missile throwers and many Scandinavians called theirs by the female name Gunhildr. This was an apt choice as in Icelandic *gunnr* and *hildr* meant "war." As early as 1330 a list of weapons at Windsor Castle included a big catapult known as "Lady Gunhilda."

Passing from crude stone-throwing engines to powder-fired weapons, the name was shortened to *gun*.

Gat

NUMEROUS new weapons were developed during the American Civil War, one of them being a precursor of the modern machine gun invented by a physician, Dr. Richard J. Gatling.

Dr. Gatling's revolutionary weapon was adopted by the Union army too late to be used but in only a few battles. News of it, however, had a significant psychological effect upon the already staggering Confederacy. Like the atomic bomb that was used in World War II, this weapon may have helped to persuade a defeated people to agree to surrender.

Decades later Alfred Henry Lewis wrote a colorful book about the Apaches of New York. Published in 1912, it includes the first known use of *gat* as a slang name for a gun. According to Lewis in the years before World War I, "Gatts is East Sidease for pistols." In 1920 a story called "Bullet 22" used the term *gat* for the first time in singular form.

A wave of gangster movies followed. In them, mobsters almost always spoke out of the corners of their mouths and called their revolvers "gats." There is no evidence that professional criminals had used the term earlier, and they most likely picked it up from the screen. By 1924 underworld figures were calling a firearm of any kind a *gat*.

Cataract

WHILE city walls afforded protection against enemies, their chief weakness lay in their entrances, which must be used in time of peace but quickly shut when attack was threatened. Some intelligent ancient Greek thought of making a door that would fit into slots. Lifted by weights, the door could be dropped in an instant in an action similar to water rushing over a cliff. Therefore the Greek equivalent of "waterfall" was used to describe the door. The Romans later borrowed the device and modified its name to *cataracta*.

For centuries the sliding door was an important defensive device. Medieval rulers abandoned the old solid type, however, and made it in the form of a heavy iron grating. Dropped in place and seen from a distance, such a cataracta gave a filmy appearance to the city gate. It was not unlike a common type of growth that obscured the pupil, or gate of the human eye, so by the sixteenth century the English called the obstructing tissue a *cataract*, but they retained the waterfall connection with the word.

Crusade

THE Rapid growth of Muslim military power created a threat to European nations of the eleventh century, and Christians wanted to drive the infidel from their Holy Land. This factor influenced the church to bless the military campaigns.

When a man left home to fight the Saracens, it was customary for him to go through a ceremony in which a priest marked his forehead with the sign of the cross. This gave sanctity to his pledge to follow his king into battle in the name of the Cross. French soldiers blessed by a priest in such manner were said to be *croisé*, that is, "crossed" or "marked with the cross." The English borrowed the ceremony but modified its name, which passed through several spellings before entering modern speech as *crusade*.

Some historians count seven separate Crusades against the Saracens; others identify nine. All of them failed, and in the thirteenth century the Holy Land was abandoned to its conquerors.

Memories of gallant campaigns waged in the name of the Cross resulted in calling any movement against evil a crusade.

Shibboleth

THE land of Gilead was once led by a wise and fierce old chief, or "judge," called Jephthah. Under his guidance his forces met those of Ephraim in battle and put them to rout. Since there was no quarter (or mercy) for the defeated, many of the Ephraimites tried to flee back to their own region, but Jephthah had anticipated this and had seized the fords of the Jordan River.

Neither army wore uniforms or insignia, so it was impossible to identify fugitives by their dress. It was common knowledge, however, that the tribesmen of central Palestine were unable to make a *sh* sound. Sentries stationed at the river were instructed to stop all who attempted to cross. Then each man was ordered to say the word *shibboleth*. Refugees from Ephraim's forces invariably pronounced it as *sibboleth*. Betrayed by their speech, they were killed by their foes.

Made famous by Bible readers of many generations, the test word of the Hebrew general came to stand for any word or phrase by which natives can identify persons from outside their district. Then the meaning expanded, and *shibboleth* came to stand for the password of a secret society or a catchword or formula of any sort.

Bracelet

THE prominence given to modern explosives obscures the role of the sword, which was the principal weapon used in some of the most decisive battles of history. Greece, the cradle of Western civilization, won all her victories through the strong arms of her swordsmen.

Hand-to-hand combat made it necessary for the ancient soldier to devise some sort of protection for his forearm, or *brachion*. Heavy leather bands were therefore devised for this purpose.

Ordinary fighting men used plain ones, but arm bands of officers were often decorated with precious metals.

Romans adopted the Greek arm band and later passed it on to Frankish warriors from the north. In their speech it was called *bracel*, and it became a standard piece of military gear. A woman who wore an ornament about her wrist came to be described as having a *bracelet* ("little bracel"). The invention of gunpowder made the fighting man's leather arm band obsolete, so its memory is preserved only in the decorative *bracelet* it named.

Medal

DURING the centuries of Rome's glory, international trade expanded to a point never reached before, creating a demand for large quantities of coins. Since the supply of precious metals was inadequate, and since coins of small value were needed, in their coinage some of the emperors used any metal they could get. Naturally, it was impossible to standardize the value of their polyglot coins that were called *metallia* ("piece of metal").

With the fall of the Roman Empire, the word seemed destined for extinction. Long afterward, European rulers hit upon the idea of striking metal discs to commemorate military victories and other events. They had no name for such objects, however, so they borrowed from the colloquial speech of the ancient Romans and called the coinlike piece a *medal*.

Persons who were awarded medals were proud of them and usually displayed them in some prominent place. So the name spread to stand for any mark of distinction, whether shaped like a coin or not.

Quota

MEDIEVAL rulers didn't find it easy to raise the funds they needed. It was a simple matter to decide on a desired total, but in order to collect it specific portions had to be assigned to various divisions of the kingdom. The portion of a tax levy assigned to a city or county was called its *quota*, from a Latin term meaning "what part."

Quota systems proved so effective that they were adopted by military leaders. In 1795 the English Parliament passed a famous quota bill that listed the exact number of men to be furnished to the Royal Navy from every county and even every port of the nation. Draft quotas imposed by Washington during the Civil War led to the most serious protest riots of the period, the best known of which brought widespread destruction and looting to New York City.

American businessmen applied the military expression to their sales territories, and it became commonplace to assign a *quota* to each salesperson who was given a territory.

Thyroid

PART of the defensive equipment for ancient Greek fighting men was a light shield, oblong in shape, closely resembling a miniature door. Therefore the soldiers of Attica called the shield *thyreoeides*, from their word for "door."

Long after this Greek gear was abandoned, its name survived to designate any shield-shaped surface—large or small. Anatomists of the seventeenth century discovered two sections of oblong cartilage in the human throat. Adapting the shield name to modern speech, they called it the "thyroid cartilage." Surgeons later became interested in a ductless gland behind these minute oblong plates. Located as it is behind the thyroid cartilage, it was inevitable that it should be called the *thyroid* gland.

Bassinet

PROTECTIVE headgear was among the most vital items in a medieval knight's equipment, so French artisans developed special basin-shaped pieces with moveable visors. From its resemblance to kitchen utensils, such a helmet was called a *bassinet* ("small basin"), and the term was adopted by their English foes.

With the rise of firearms many technical labels for armor dropped from speech. They had a colorful revival, however, in the romantic novels of Sir Walter Scott and his imitators. Folk who read about dashing heroes with basinlike helmets were inspired to compare the armor with a kind of wicker baby's basket of similar shape. Once firmly attached to nursery gear, the name *bassinet* has stuck in spite of sweeping changes in styles.

Budget

STRUGGLING with a budget is no new problem; it dates back to the days of the Roman Empire. Housewives had to be cautious in their spending. They kept money for household expenses in a little leather *bulga* (Latin for "bag"). This custom also prevailed among businessmen, who may have borrowed it from their wives or vice versa. Centuries later, the Latin word was adopted into Middle French as *bougette* ("little leather bag"). When the British Chancellor of Exchequer appeared before Parliament, he carried his papers explaining the estimated revenue and expenses in a leather bag and then "opened the budget" for the coming year. Thus *budget* (as it came to be pronounced) came to mean a systematic plan for expenditures, both for governments and for private individuals.

First Rate

DURING the heyday of her naval expansion, Britain set up an elaborate system of classification. Every warship she owned was inspected and placed in a category, or rate, which was determined by the number and weight of the guns she mounted. There were six of these rates, and members of the Royal Navy measured their prestige by the rate of their vessel. Every officer hoped to command, some day, a ship of the first rate. Standing as it did for the mightiest vessels afloat, *first rate* came to be used for anything high in quality, whether on sea or land.

Dreadnought

DURING the early years of the twentieth century, England was determined to preserve her place as mistress of the seas, no matter what the cost. Her experts constantly devised new types of ships, heavier guns, and thicker armament.

In 1907 it seemed that builders of warships had reached the ultimate. That year Britain launched a battleship armed with ten twelve-inch guns. As the largest warship in the world, she had a displacement of 17,900 tons and a speed of twenty-one knots.

His Majesty's sailors bragged that the new vessel feared nothing that sailed the seas. Smugly, they named her H.M.S. *Dreadnought.* In popular use, battleships of all navies were soon called dreadnoughts. Later generations used the term loosely, applying it to any powerful individual.

CHAPTER 8

HOUSEHOLD

HARD-BOILED

BISCUIT

BAY WINDOW

RUMMAGE

GUMBO

BRING HOME THE BACON

FLOUR

EAT ONE'S HAT

LORD

MAKE NO BONES

CRUST

BUTTER

MARMALADE

CHEESE

MUG

COOKING TERMS

SHORTENING

LADY

SUNDAE

VEGETABLES

TABLEWARE

BORN WITH A SILVER
  SPOON IN ONE'S
  MOUTH

FRUIT NAMES

BREAD-AND-BUTTER
  NOTE

COMPANION

CURFEW

X FOR KISS

BEAU

BLOCKHEAD

BUCKLE

BURLAP

CHAPERONE

DOUBLE-DYED

LINGERIE

MAD AS A HATTER

NEGLIGEE

PETTICOAT

SPINSTER

NEEDLE

THROW DOWN THE
  GAUNTLET

WIDOW'S PEAK

Hard-Boiled

HARD-BOILED persons get their title—not from likeness to a cooked egg, but from washday habits of American pioneers. Homemakers of frontier days used lye soap and often washed in an open stream. Clothes tended to gray very quickly, so at least once a month the fastidious woman boiled her wash in a black iron pot. Then she starched the best pieces with a paste made in her own kitchen.

She sometimes got her husband's Sunday shirts too stiff. Trying to make the best of the situation, he would jokingly accuse his wife of having boiled the clothes so long they became hard. Passing from stiffly starched clothing, the colorful term attached to people; and the *hard-boiled* American emerged as a callous, unfeeling, tough person.

Biscuit

PRIMITIVE navigators stayed close to the coast, but by Roman times a few hardy sailors were venturing into the open sea where they found the problem of food supply to be acute.

There were no cooking facilities on early wooden vessels, so it was necessary to carry along a supply of bread baked on shore. This was highly unsatisfactory, for the bread quickly became moldy and inedible.

A baker discovered that by reheating thin cakes of unleavened bread he could drive out the moisture and make it suitable for use on voyages. Such pastry was called *bis coctus*, from the Latin for "twice-cooked." Centuries later, with the original meaning forgotten, the name evolved into *biscuit*—closely related to Italian *biscotti*, increasingly available in American groceries and coffee shops of the twenty-first century. German *zwieback*, which literally means "twice baked," also preserves the original meaning.

Bay Window

AT least as early as the fourteenth century, architects devised a novel type of window. Projecting outward from the wall of the house, it is sometimes made as a rectangle and sometimes as a semicircle. Because it gave a room a recess like a tiny harbor, or bay, sailors called it a *bay window*.

In America in the 1890s some imaginative person transferred its name to the bulging human paunch.

Rummage

FEW operations require more skill than that of loading a large ship. There is a vast amount of space, and every part of it must be packed tightly. Otherwise, the motion of the vessel might cause the cargo to break loose and shift, causing damage at least, or the ship to sink at worst.

Early French shippers adopted a special term for the loading operation. Their word was *arrumage*, related to the ancestor of "arrange," and it was used to indicate the packing of lumber, casks, and other heavy articles in the hold of a vessel. No matter how carefully the job was done, however, experience proved that some of the cargo was sure to get damaged.

Warehouses frequently put such goods to one side until enough accumulated for a special sale. These goods came to be called "rummage." By the fifteenth century the word was being applied to any collection of goods of low quality. Now the *rummage* sale has come to be associated with clothing and other items householders sell to earn a little money.

Gumbo

GUMBO is one of the few English words that originated in Africa. It is a thick soup or stew based on a roux, thickened with okra pods, and served over rice. The African okra plant was called *ngombo* by the Bantu tribe in northern Angola. Travelers and explorers became acquainted with the *ngombo* plant as early as 1700. They found natives using its stems for rope fiber, but regarded the plant as a botanical curiosity.

When the slave trade boomed in the seventeenth and eighteenth centuries, hundreds of thousands of Africans were shipped to the United States. By 1790 there were 200,000 slaves in Virginia alone. Inevitably, some of these slaves were Bantu, and with them came some *ngombo* seeds. Soon slaves were extensively cultivating the plant, and the plant name was shortened to "gumbo." At first their masters refused to taste the thick soup made from gumbo; it was as sticky as a red-clay hill after a nightlong rain. By the time whites cultivated a taste for the novel dish, its name was firmly attached to miry soil.

Polite white society frowned on Negro words and succeeded in substituting "okra" for the older slave name. In recent decades the term has re-emerged and *gumbo* is now widely familiar despite the fact that its colorful history is not widely known.

Bring Home the Bacon

THIS expression for success in competition came into vogue from a prize given for happy marriages. At the church of Dunmow, in Essex County, England, a flitch of bacon used to be given annually to the man and woman who, after a year of matrimony, were judged to have lived in greatest harmony and fidelity. The earliest recorded case of the awarding of the bacon took place in 1445.

By the end of the sixteenth century, couples who came forward to seek the prize were questioned before a jury of six bachelors and six maidens. Only those who gave satisfactory proof of domestic felicity gained the coveted pork. It was awarded at irregular intervals until late in the nineteenth century.

Widely publicized in literature, the fact that successful claimants actually did *bring home the bacon* from Dunmow led to the application of the phrase to victory in general.

Flour

DURING the Elizabethan Age the word "flower" meant "the best," as it does today in such expressions as "the flower of our nation's youth."

Millers of the period ground wheat by a crude process, then sifted their meal. Only the finest of it passed through the cloth sieve. Reserved for tables of the nobility, this top-quality ground wheat was naturally called the "flower of wheat," but in this context the word came to be spelled *flour*. The two spellings were used interchangeably until the nineteenth century. In *Paradise Lost* Milton wrote the line, "O flours that never will in other climates grow."

Eat One's Hat

MANY a man engaged in a contest of some sort has offered to eat his hat if he loses. In such a situation a knowledge of etymology would be of great value — for the expression *eat one's hat* once referred not to a Stetson or a Panama, but to a culinary product.

Napier's famous *Boke of Cookry*, one of the earliest European cookbooks, gives the following directions: "Hattes are made of eggs, veal, dates, saffron, salt, and so forth." In the hands of amateur cooks, the concoction was frequently so unpalatable that it required a strong stomach to eat it.

Even so, the early braggart who offered to eat a hatte had in mind nothing so distasteful as a felt or a straw.

Lord

BREAD was literally "the staff of life" for centuries. When the grain crop was good, people grew fat and prosperous; when it was bad, they grew thin and starved. Hence, community and family life revolved around bread.

In Anglo-Saxon households the most powerful male was responsible for guarding the bread supply. He even had a formal title, *hlafweard* ("loaf keeper"). This gradually contracted and emerged into modern English as *lord*.

Make No Bones

ELABORATE menus were unknown to the common people of medieval Europe. Cooking vessels were rare and expensive, so vegetables were usually boiled in a single pot. Unless a housewife had a piece of meat large enough to roast, she usually tossed it in with her turnips, beans, cabbage, and carrots. Often a pot of stew included the neck, wings, and feet from a fowl or two.

Frequently a pot boiled for hours. Bones separated and became dispersed throughout the stew. This made it customary to eat with some degree of caution, removing the bones that were found. In addition to these real bones, fearful persons frequently gagged on imaginary ones. As a result, by 1450 a person making objections or showing hesitation of any sort was said to be "finding bones."

This expression came into such wide use that people needed an equally forceful way of describing an opposite attitude. They found it by saying that those who plunge boldly into an undertaking *make no bones* about it.

Crust

THE Romans who lived in the time of Julius Caesar used *crusta* to stand for any type of hard shell. That is why hard-shelled creatures such as crabs and lobsters are still called "crustaceans." After the Roman Empire fell, vulgar (everyday) Latin evolved into today's romance languages — Italian, Spanish, Portuguese, Romanian, and French. Passing through Old French, *crusta* reached England via the Norman Conquest and became "crust."

At least one written instance of the word dates from the period when King Edward III was preparing to extend England's holdings on the European continent. By then, many bakers prided themselves upon skill in making a thick, hard crust. Wrapping paper had not been invented, and a good crust served to protect the loaf from dirt and insects. The soft bread inside the crust was usually called the "crumb," and sometimes remained fresh and tasty for surprisingly long periods of time. Much later an irritable person was compared with an over-baked loaf and called "crusty," or short-tempered.

Butter

GREEK farmers began keeping cattle long before Philip of Macedon built his great empire in the fourth century B.C. Both the ox and the cow were known as *bous* — a word still surviving in "bossy." Milk from the *bous* was more difficult to keep than goats' milk; when a skin of it was agitated, bits of hardened fat rose to the surface. From the name of the animal that produced it, the substance was called *boutyron*.

Caesar's legionnaires adopted this term from the Greeks whom they conquered and took it with them when they invaded distant Britain. There it replaced the native name and was modified into *butter*. The early English kept few cows but made considerable butter from ewe's milk. Salted, it became a major food item for use on sailing vessels. By the fourteenth century butter was common enough to be familiar to most householders. It became an important article of commerce only when modern dairies put the family cow out of business.

Marmalade

BEFORE the rise of the Roman Empire, a Greek gardener experimented in grafting fruit trees. Using sturdy wild quince stock and a variety of apples, he produced a delicacy so sweet that it came to be called the *melimelon*, or "honey apple." Passing through Latin, the name of the exotic fruit entered Portuguese as *marmelo*, which was a quince.

Due to its texture and acid content, the marmelo proved ideal for making preserves. Boiled with sugar, it yielded a confection the Portuguese called *marmelada*. English travelers became familiar with the delicacy and began importing it as a luxury. In 1524 Hull of Exeter presented a box of the delicacy to King Henry VIII.

Known to the English as *marmalade*, the tasty preserve is usually made from the pulp and rind of citrus fruits.

Cheese

AN accident may have been responsible for the world's first cheese. Instead of storing the day's milk in a good, tight skin, some ancient housewife may have poured it in a well-worn bag. When she returned, she found the liquid portion of her milk had seeped through seams and tiny holes, leaving a tasty solid behind.

Eventually, the solidified milk was called *caseus* by the Romans because it was made by hanging the liquid in a thin bag, or case. Armies of occupation took the milk product with them into conquered lands—including Britain. Modified by centuries of oral transmission, its name emerged into modern English as *cheese*.

At least a century before Columbus sailed for the New World, farm folk had learned how to mold the food into balls and cakes. In such form the rind provided a natural cover that made it possible to ship cheese long distances. Hence, it was one of the earliest food products to be sold by retail merchants. Today there are literally thousands of cheeses, called after the places where they are made.

Mug

OUR custom of referring to the human face as a mug is of relatively recent origin. Many beer mugs of the eighteenth century were shaped to represent grotesque human heads. A person not particularly noted for beauty of feature might bear a more-than-superficial resemblance to faces on such mugs. Consequently, he would receive much joshing about his ugly *mug* from friends and associates.

Cooking Terms

THERE is at least one serious gap in European history. Her contemporaries failed to record the name of the woman who first thought of stuffing an egg. Nothing is known about her recipe, except that she was liberal with pepper. Her invention was so hot that folk who tried it were reminded of Beelzebub's fiery furnaces. As a result the tidbit came to be called a *deviled egg*.

Most other terms of cookery are prosaic by comparison. More than half were borrowed from the French—which suggests that English cooks were never very imaginative.

Braise stems from French for "hot charcoal." *Toast* is but slightly modified from *toaster* ("to parch with heat"). *Boil* stems from a continental verb meaning "to make little bubbles." *Poach* grew out of *pocher*, which meant "to pouch"— that is, to enclose an egg's yellow in a little pouch of white. *Fry, grill, roast*, and *baste* were also adapted from French. *Fricassee* was taken as is from that language, but its ultimate origin is unknown.

The oldest term in cookery is probably *cook*, still much like Latin *coquus*. The Norse gave us *bake*, from *baka* ("hearth"). The Saxons contributed *sear*, spelled just as it is today. It originally meant "to wither by heat." *Scorch*—bane of a cook's existence—

has a long history that goes all the way back to the Old English *scorkle*, which started life as a term for skinning meat by searing.

Shortening

ENGLAND'S textile trade was at a low ebb during the early Middle Ages. Centuries of inbreeding had produced flocks of sheep that grew very short wool. Limited to the use of such wool, even the most skillful of weavers could not make first-quality cloth. It tore easily and tended to come apart in use. Nevertheless, so much of the wool was produced that people began referring to any flimsy material as "made of short wool." In time the expression was abbreviated to "short."

Most bread of the era was baked extremely hard. Then housewives discovered that the liberal use of butter or lard made bread light or flaky—like short cloth. Consequently, the ingredient that made such a change in cooking came to be called *shortening*. A cookbook written in 1430 gives one of the first formal recipes for making shortbread.

Lady

IN Anglo-Saxon times most families were quite large, so there was much work to be done around the household. Custom decreed that special tasks should be allotted to various female members of the group.

Unmarried girls usually looked after such matters as milking and spinning. But the privilege of making bread, one of the most important items of their diet, was reserved by the housewife herself. She was called the *lae-dige*, meaning "the bread kneader." Later centuries modified the term to *lady*. Etymologically speaking, no woman is entitled to be called a lady until she has learned to make bread!

Sundae

NUMEROUS stories are told concerning the origin of the ice-cream sundae, differing chiefly in tracing it to various American cities. There seems little doubt that the basic account is accurate. Evidence points to Evanston, Illinois, as the city of origin. It seems that around 1875, city fathers passed a law forbidding the sale of ice-cream sodas on Sunday. Someone thought of serving ice cream with syrup but no soda water.

This "Sunday soda" became quite popular, and on weekdays numbers of customers asked for "Sundays." Officials of the city objected to naming the dish after the Sabbath, so the spelling was modified—and *sundae* it has been ever since.

Vegetables

SINCE ancient times gardeners have cultivated a pungent little tuber that will grow in almost any soil. Its English name is not so old, however. Adopted as *radish*, it comes from the medieval French *radis,* a name modified from a word meaning "root."

Like the wart-shaped root, many vegetables were named for particular qualities. *Lettuce* evolved from *lactuca*, Latin for "the milk-giving plant." *Corn* goes back to a Saxon word, *korn,* thought to be derived from an expression for "a worn-down particle." *Cabbage* stems from the French *cubic* ("head"). *Broccoli*, an import from Italy, took its name from *bronco*, or "little spike."

We get other vegetable names from various modern tongues. *Gherkin* is Dutch for "small cucumber." *Potato* was first *patata* in Spanish after the Haitian name *batata*. *Rutabaga* is a Swedish version of "turnip." The plant from Mexico called *tomate* by the Spanish entered English as *tomato*, and the uncooked gourd *asquutasquash* of the American Indian became streamlined to *squash*. *Asparagus* was adapted by Romans from a Persian word for "sprout." A French term for "round," helped to name the round root—or *turnip. Mushroom* is also borrowed from the French, who first cultivated them in beds of *mousse* ("moss"). *Pumpkin* came through French from a Greek ancestor that meant "cooked by the sun."

Numerous vegetable names are so ancient that their names cannot be traced. Carrots, beets, and cucumbers fall in this class, as do peas, artichokes, and celery. By comparison with these old-timers, the *cantaloupe* is a youngster. Europeans first became acquainted with it when it was brought from Armenia to Cantaloupo, a country estate near Rome that at the time was owned by the pope.

Tableware

No matter how fashionable your tableware may be, every piece of it is more than five hundred years old—at least in name.

That essential tool, the *fork,* is the youngest of the lot. It takes its name from Latin *furca*, or "farmer's pitchfork." Miniature versions of the ancient tool didn't come into table use until the fifteenth century. *Spoon* is a modern version of Anglo-Saxon *spon*—which meant "chip," or "thin piece of wood." Clearly, porridge was once dipped with a chip. *Knife* is so old that its origin is lost because it can't be traced beyond the Old English *cnif.*

Several standard pieces received their names from their shapes. A *dish* still resembles the Roman discus, which athletes hurled in their national games. *Bowl* comes from Anglo-Saxon *bolla* ("round"). Old French *plat* ("flat") left its imprint upon both the *plate* and the *platter.*

Its composition gave the *tureen* its name. Medieval French housewives called it *terrine*, since it was made of "terre," or clay. *Calabash,* also borrowed from the French, started life as a Persian term for "gourd."

The *cup* is the oldest household drinking vessel, whose ancestral name was probably the Sanskrit *kupa* ("little well"). *Glass* comes from an ancient source, perhaps the Celtic *glas* ("green")— the color of the first crude glass. An early *tumbler* did just what its name suggests. It was made with a round bottom and so tumbled over unless inverted. *Goblet* is a French importation of uncertain ancestry; the first such tableware may have been produced by an artisan whose surname was Gobel.

Finally, the *saucer* has a delightful history. For many generations it was a special dish for holding "sauce," or salt. Although the
name was used as early as 1340, only the machine age made
saucers common enough to be used under cups.

Born with a Silver Spoon in One's Mouth

TABLE utensils of silver—sterling or plated—have become
commonplace only in recent times. As late as 1800 only the upper
classes owned eating utensils of precious metal. Housewives of the
middle and lower economic classes had to be content with pewter.

Earlier generations didn't have metal tableware of any sort.
That's shown by the word *spoon*, which grew out of the Anglo-
Saxon *spon* ("chip"). Obviously, the earliest spoons were made of
wood. Artisans later discovered how to fashion them from horns of
domestic animals. Even among the nobility, metal spoons were not
in wide use before the Elizabethan Age.

After precious metals came into limited use for table utensils,
wealthy persons adopted the practice of giving silver spoons to their
godchildren. The gifts were formally presented at the christening
ceremonies, which usually took place when infants were only a few
days old. That made it natural to refer to one who received such a
gift as being born with a silver spoon in one's mouth. A few generations of use impressed the phrase so strongly that it came to stand
for prosperity or wealth gained by accident of birth.

Fruit Names

WHEN a certain fruit tree was imported from Persia by the
Greeks, fruit from the "Persian tree" was known as *perspicua*.
Passing through several languages, the name entered English as
peach. Centuries later, around 100 B.C., a Roman general discovered another delicacy that grew in Cerasos, a city of Pontus, a
Roman province on the south shore of the Black Sea. Soon it was
being shipped to Rome for imperial banquets. Called *cerasus,* it

eventually became *cerise* in France and *cherry* in England. This type of name formation was repeated when oranges from Tangier, in Morocco, came to be known as *tangerines*.

Ancient bedouins called one of their favorite fruits *al-birquq* ("the early-ripener"). Passing through Portuguese to French to English, the name became *apricot*. Both the *date* and the *banana* are so called because they are shaped somewhat like a human finger. The former term evolved from *dactylus*, the Greek word for "finger," and the latter developed when traders mistook an African word for the Arabic *banan* ("finger"). A similar misunderstanding gave the *avocado* its name. When Spanish adventurers in Mexico asked the Aztecs what it was called, the natives said *ahuacatl*, their word for "testicle"; they thought it resembled the organ and excited sexual activity. To the Spanish it sounded a bit like "avocado," Spanish for "advocate." Once bestowed, the name stuck.

Bread-and-Butter Note

EXCEPT for the privileged classes, persons of the 1700s usually had little variety in their food, and bread and butter were staple fare. Someone feeding a stranger was said to furnish his bread and butter, in the same sense that a man would take a job to earn his bread and butter. When a house guest left, it was customary to write a letter thanking the hostess for the food and lodging.

Such a *bread-and-butter note* came to be standard. By 1900 American usage made the expression stand for a conventional thank-you for any sort of hospitality—even when nothing remotely resembling bread and butter is served.

Companion

SOUTHERN hospitality has come to be held in wide esteem, yet the people of Dixie have seldom approached the standards that prevailed for centuries in the Near East.

It was an unwritten law that the householder must open his

doors to any traveler who desired food and shelter. Chance encounters might bring men together only once in their lives, but the act of eating together was concluded by a vow of undying friendship.

Eating about a common table was almost religious in nature. This attitude carried over into Roman times. To do evil to a man after breaking bread with him was considered treachery of the highest order. Our word *companion* is a monument to that view. Almost without change it comes to us from the Latin *com* ("together") and *panis* ("bread"). In the literal etymological sense, only persons who have eaten bread together are companions.

Curfew

FIRE was a fearful enemy of the early medieval householder. Cottages were generally made of wood and were built right next to each other on the edge of a forest or in a small clearing. If fire broke out in the forest or a cottage, it wouldn't take long to spread, destroying an entire village.

In winter men could not work in a wood or field without a nearby brush fire at which to occasionally warm themselves. So long as every man extinguished his blaze when he quit work for the day, danger was minimized. Some were too lazy or indifferent, however, so royal proclamations made it mandatory to cover every open fire at dusk. Village church bells, audible for several miles, tolled the signal for *couvre feu* ("cover fire").

The English slurred the Norman-French term into *curfew*. Later the term came to be attached to requirements that persons be in their homes by a particular hour of the day.

X for Kiss

OUR custom of putting *X*s at the end of letters to symbolize kisses grew out of medieval legal practices. In order to indicate good faith and honesty, the sign of Saint Andrew was placed after the signature on all important documents. This sign is quite like the letter *x*.

Contracts and agreements were not considered binding until each signer added Saint Andrew's cross after his name. Then he was required to kiss it to guarantee the faithful performance of his obligations.

Over the centuries the origin of the ceremony was forgotten. People associated *x* with the kiss instead of the pledge of good faith, and the modern custom was born.

Beau

FROM a Latin term for "good, fine, or beautiful," medieval Frenchmen made great use of the word *beau*. One of the many expressions in which it appeared was "le beau monde," meaning the beautiful world. A fop or dandy, one of the "beautiful people," became a *beau*.

This usage was well established across the English Channel, so in the eighteenth century it was natural for the self-styled master of ceremonies at Bath, England's most fashionable spa, to apply the title to himself. As the "arbiter of elegance," Beau Nash, once tore a lace apron off a duchess, declaring she looked like a servant.

With the passing of the professional dandy the title expanded in meaning. As a result, whether or not he is good, fine, or handsome, any attendant or suitor is often termed a *beau* in the twenty-first century.

Blockhead

UNTIL the 1300s few English men or women except members of the nobility wore hats. Then hoods went out of fashion in the space of two or three generations, and all sorts of men began wearing hats of leather and felt. Some of the most popular styles were shaped like thimbles, while other styles resembled sugar loaves.

Hat makers multiplied and formed guilds in which expert craftsmen became adept at pleasing their customers—almost all of whom were males. They learned how to make imitation beaver from goat's wool and how to use head-shaped blocks of yew or oak in forming hats that fit snugly and held their shape.

In time such "block heads" became standard gear among hatters. By the time Henry VIII ascended the throne, dull-witted persons were being compared with dummy heads in hat shops. As a result it became standard usage to label a dolt or simpleton a *blockhead*.

Buckle

From the beginning of organized warfare, fighting men have had special problems in protecting their heads. Before 500 B.C. Greek hoplites wore elaborate bronze helmets that not only protected the skull but were also equipped with cheek pieces and nasal strips.

The Romans seem to have made only one major change. Because a man was all but doomed if he had his helmet knocked off in battle, a retaining strap was devised and held in place by a clamp. Resting as it did near the cheek piece, the strap holder was called a *buccula* ("cheek").

The basic idea and the name *buckle* were adapted to various other articles of clothing. By 1340 the fastener was being used as what a well-dressed woman demurely termed the "bocle of ye gerdle." Today the clasp devised for Roman legionnaires serves on everything from airplane seat belts to a cowboy's belt.

Burlap

For many centuries European farmers had more success with flax than any other cultivated fiber. German housewives perfected various types of linen and even managed to salvage coarse strands that could not be used in better-grade fabrics. Cloth made from such stuff was coarse, stiff, and rubbed the skin of its wearer. It took a special name compounded from *boen* ("rubbing") and *lap* ("linen").

Introduced to Britain, the name *boenlap* became *burlap*. Subsequent generations saw the rise of modern commerce and the introduction of such new fibers as hemp and jute. Fabrics made from these coarse materials took the name of the old rough linen and became prominent in the manufacture of bags and baling material. In spite of changes in both spelling and fiber, anyone wearing a garment of modern burlap would find that the fabric still qualifies as "rubbing cloth."

Chaperone

FRENCH priests and others in the early Middle Ages wore a special type of hood, which they called a *chaperon*, meaning "little mantle." This hood crossed the English Channel with the Norman Conquest and was long worn only by men. Edward III made the chaperon part of the full-dress costume worn by members of the Order of the Garter when he founded it in 1349.

In the same spirit that led modern women to adopt slacks, medieval ladies began to wear their lords' chaperone. For more than a century the garment was fashionable. Then it fell into disuse, and only old ladies who cared nothing about fashion continued to wear it. They were the sort often designated to watch over young girls. As late as 1830 it was said that any attractive miss was likely to be guarded by an old witch wearing a chaperon.

Eventually the garment disappeared, but its name stuck to guardians of conduct with the result that the *chaperone* was a fixture of American life until recent times.

Double-Dyed

UNTIL the modern chemical industry made colorful dyes plentiful, housewives had many problems in trying to make brightly colored clothing. They dyed their own homemade fabrics, often using juices squeezed from native plants. Color fixation was so poor that it became common to dry the material, then send it back through the vat. Such double-dyed cloth could be identified almost at a glance.

Lawyers and judges, searching for an expression to designate a hardened criminal, borrowed from the vocabulary of their wives. Consequently any person deeply stained with guilt came to be called a *double-dyed* rogue or scoundrel.

Lingerie

AS late as the Victorian era good-quality cloth was costly. Only natural fibers were used, so there was a definite limit to variety in weave and texture. French designers won international fame by creating distinctive garments from commonplace fabric. From ordinary linen (*linge*) they made exquisite linen dresses (*lingerie*) for special occasions.

Although women had more and more choices in outerdress fabrics, they continued to like the feel of soft lingerie next to their skin. Thus the name became attached only to intimate wear, even though it is now more likely to be produced from man-made fibers.

Mad as a Hatter

THE Mad Hatter in *Alice's Adventures in Wonderland* is a well known literary character. What is not so well known is that there were lots of mad hatters in England before the invention of a felt-making machine in 1846.

A popular fabric for hats, felt is made of wool fibers or animal hair matted together. Mercuric nitrate was used in the process and long-time exposure to this caused hat makers to have twitching muscles, a lurching gait, incoherent speech, and confused minds. In those days people considered them insane, or mad. Thus the phrase *mad as a hatter* entered the language.

Negligee

FRENCH society reached heights of extravagance and ostentation under Louis XIV. Ladies were expected to spend hours dressing themselves before any formal occasion. Sometimes this pomp and ceremony lost its zest. Many a beauty dressed casually in the privacy of her own rooms at the cost of being criticized for her *négligé* ("neglected") attire.

Designers eventually created loose, comfortable dresses for periods of relaxation. Naturally they took the name by which informal clothing was already designated. In this form the negligee was popular for more than a century and was associated in popular thought with uninhibited conduct in rather intimate surroundings. Gradually *negligee* took on the more limited meaning of a loose dressing gown.

Petticoat

IT was normal in the Middle Ages for a man to wear a petticoat. When knights wore armor their bodies needed protection against chafing at the shoulders and the unpleasantness of very cold or hot metal.

Therefore, an ingenious tailor conceived the idea of making a short, snug, padded coat to wear under the coat of mail. Because such a garment was smaller than the ordinary coat, it was termed a "petty-coat." Soldiers were loud in their praise of the petty-coat.

Civilian men began to wear them under their doublets and women under their dresses. Over a period of centuries the *petticoat* was restricted to a woman's underskirt.

Spinster

OUR word "spinster," meaning an unmarried woman, is rapidly becoming archaic and is likely to drop out of speech during the twenty-first century.

The term hasn't always had the application now attached to it. The original use applied to the occupation of spinning, which was traditionally a woman's job. In the ninth century King Alfred spoke of his descendants as those on the spear side and the spindle side—that is, male and female. "Spinster" was widely used as a title of respect for both single and married women until the time of Queen Elizabeth.

Since homemakers with families had to take on other responsibilities, spinning became more and more the occupation of unmarried women. By the seventeenth century practically all professional spinsters were unmarried. So, in the course of time, it came to be natural that women not likely to marry should be called *spinsters*.

Needle

AS late as the beginning of the nineteenth century, most fashionable garments were hand-sewn. Tailors often worked in shops, and seamstresses worked at home.

Plying the needle many hours each day, even veteran sewers pricked themselves frequently. Though commonplace, such an occurrence was always annoying. So it was not strange that when a man was stuck, he should heap abuse upon his needle. Sore thumbs were so abundant among tailors that any cause of irritation was said to *needle* its victim.

Throw Down the Gauntlet

KNIGHTS of the age of chivalry were seldom so gallant and noble as they appear in the pages of romances. Many of them were rough, brawling fellows who divided their time between boasting, tippling, and fighting.

As long as opponents used only verbal abuse, there was no certainty that blows would be exchanged. When a man meant business and really wanted to cross swords with a foe, he indicated it by throwing his metal-plated leather glove, or gauntlet, to the ground. This constituted his "gage" or promise of battle.

There are indications that blustering was more common than mortal combat. Still, the custom made sufficient impact to affect general speech. By the time Sir Francis Drake sailed around the globe late in the 1500s, the use of armored gloves had been abandoned, but the expression survives, so to *throw down the gauntlet* still indicates any act of serious challenge.

Widow's Peak

IN the Middle Ages custom, and sometimes law, required that particular garments be worn by persons in various occupations. There was even an ironclad dictum that widows wear special garb.

One of the most distinctive features of this somber outfit was the pointed hood, or peak. It was unlike any other headgear of the period; one could glance at it and know the wearer to be a widow.

The emancipation of women made special clothing of the widow obsolete, but the pointed hood left an indelible impression upon our language. Any person whose hair grows to a point in the middle of the forehead is still said to have a *widow's peak*.

CHAPTER 9

CRITTERS AND FAMOUS PEOPLE

BIGHEAD

PEDIGREE

PIE

NAMES OF PERSONS

CROW TO PICK

HOLD A CANDLE

WHOLE HOG

THE OX IS IN THE DITCH

A PRETTY PENNY

GREASE ONE'S PALM

FEELING ONE'S OATS

PEG OUT

SLIPSHOD

CAJOLE

GUTTERSNIPE

HAIL FELLOW WELL
    MET

Bighead

COLLOQUIAL speech describes a conceited person as afflicted with big head. This sounds like an allusion to a real or fancied abundance of gray matter. However, the word originated among cattle farmers.

Ranchers who penetrated the Mississippi Valley found the grass long and green—but sprinkled in with it was Saint-John's-wort. When eaten in quantity, this herb caused severe inflammation of the bones—especially the skull.

Scientists referred to the malady as osteoporosis; pioneers used the much more vivid term *bighead*. The disease struck horses and sheep as well as cattle. So common was the disease that by 1850 its name was being used to stand for humans who behaved as though they were afflicted with a case of sore head.

Pedigree

WHEN we boast of a distinguished pedigree, we are actually speaking of a crane's foot.

Medieval French genealogists used a three-pronged mark to show lines of descent. Such a symbol resembled the imprint of a crane's foot, so it came to be called *pied de grue* ("foot of the crane") and was used both for the symbol and for the ancestral line.

English genealogists borrowed both the symbol and its name, but the pronunciation and then the spelling emerged as *pedigree*.

Pie

UNTIL the 1700s the bird now known as the "magpie" was called simply "pie." Then as now, the bird was likely to be a habitual collector, and it was not unusual to find a pie's nest filled with an assortment of pebbles, bits of broken glass, string, chicken feathers, and so on.

At some unrecorded time housewives thought of placing a crust around a small pot of stew. They used whatever ingredients were at hand—meat, fowl, or fish, plus a few vegetables and perhaps an egg or two. Menfolk liked the conglomeration, and someone compared it with a pie's nest filled with odds and ends, so the dish was called a *pie*.

First used in writing about 1303, the word came to include many varieties of pie.

Names of Persons

Saxophone / Diesel / Macadamize / Blanket /
Nicotine / Mansard / Ferris Wheel / Watt/
Volt / Pasteurize / Galvanized / Fahrenheit / Camel's Hair

NUMEROUS everyday words perpetuate the names of inventors and discoverers. Saxophone commemorates Joseph Sax, the Belgian musician who invented it; *diesel* is from Rudolph Diesel, the inventor; *macadamize* comes from John L. McAdam, a Scot who disliked muddy roads and discovered a new kind of surface for them; and *blankets* immortalize Thomas Blanket, who set up the first loom for their manufacture in 1340.

Because Jacques Nicot introduced tobacco into France in 1560, we have the word *nicotine*. François Mansart developed the *mansard* roof, and the *Ferris wheel* was designed by George Washington Ferris.

When you buy a sixty-*watt* bulb, you honor James Watt, a Scottish engineer. *Volt* comes from Count Alessandro Volta; *pasteurize* is from Louis Pasteur; and anything made of *galvanized* metal commemorates Luigi Galvani. We even measure temperature by a man's surname, that of the physicist, Gabriel Fahrenheit.

Camel's-hair brushes do not come from camels; they are made from the hair of squirrels' tails! A German artist, Kemul, was the first to tie up the hair of that animal for use as paint brushes, and the term *camel's hair* is a corruption of "Kemul's hair."

Crow to Pick

THE common folk of England fared hard after the Normans conquered the island in the eleventh century. Game animals had been a major source of meat, but now the rulers claimed many of the great forests and made it illegal for peasants to hunt such animals as deer and boar. Most game birds were also reserved for the tables of the nobility.

This forced lower-class persons to eat coarse and undesirable foods.

In desperation they even began hunting crows. These birds were large and plump, but it was a major operation to pluck all the tiny black feathers from one of them; usually two persons worked together at the task. Dislike for crow picking was so widespread that when anyone had a disagreeable matter to settle with his neighbor, it became proverbial that he had *a crow to pick* with him.

Hold a Candle

IT was common in the sixteenth century and later for servants holding candles to guide their masters along the poorly lighted streets of English cities. Theaters also employed candle-holders, called "link-boys," in the days before gas lighting.

Candle-holding was among the most menial of jobs, but some poor wights failed at them for not knowing the roads or the layout of a theater, and they were said to be *not worthy to hold a candle to anyone*. This expression soon came to be used in the sense of comparing abilities of two people.

Whole Hog

FEW animals have made so large a contribution to mankind as has the sheep. For centuries such countries as England and Scotland depended upon sheep, not only for food and clothing, but also as a chief commodity in international trade. In the case of individual farmers, life frequently revolved about their flocks.

Minute attention was paid to every phase of the sheep's development, and a large special vocabulary was formed. Among the technical terms of the shepherd was "hog," which stood for an animal older than a lamb but never shorn. Fleece on a hog was short, and the first shearing was a difficult task.

Many herdsmen were careless in clipping their hogs, which became sheep after the operation. Other wool producers made it a practice to *go the whole hog*, or shear young animals with care. Spreading from the farm, the technical expression came into general use to mean "doing a thing thoroughly."

The Ox Is in the Ditch

THIS expression originated before the beginning of written history. Ancient Hebrew law included strict prohibition of labor on the Sabbath. The chief work animal of the time was the ox, whose clumsiness and stupidity frequently led to trouble. Drainage ditches and shallow wells dotted the countryside, and adventurous oxen frequently fell into them. Consequently, from sheer necessity the householder sometimes had to rescue an animal on the Sabbath.

The legal code made it permissible to do Sabbath-day work occasioned by an ox having fallen in the ditch. Other emergencies arose, such as the necessity of gathering grain or hay on the holy day. In such instances the farmer would say, *"The ox is in the ditch,"* and go about his work. As an excuse for action prohibited by conventions of society, the phrase has spread over the entire world.

A Pretty Penny

WHEN a person wants something very badly indeed, he is likely to say, "I'd give a pretty penny for that!" Since there is nothing pretty about an ordinary one-cent piece, the expression hints at a story.

Actually there once was a pretty penny—a gold piece coined in 1257, with the value of twenty shillings. King Henry III was responsible for its issue. One of the most colorful of early English kings, he showed such partiality to foreigners that his subjects staged a rebellion. Henry was relieved of power and eventually forced to turn the crown over to his son Edward. Since none of his successors wished to endorse any of Henry's practices, no additional gold pence were coined.

For several centuries tradesmen occasionally saw one of the old pieces. In addition to their intrinsic worth the gold pence came to be prized as good-luck pieces. It was natural that the shiny gold penny should be regarded as pretty, so when people wished to describe a valuable article, they spoke of it as worth *a pretty penny.*

Grease One's Palm

MOST modern women spend more time and money on adornment of the body than do men, but for centuries the reverse was true. Kings, knights, and gallants of the Age of Chivalry prided themselves on their appearance as much as on their valor. Soap was almost unheard of, however, so doughty fellows made lavish use of perfumed and spiced goose grease. Charcoal was sometimes added to give the user's skin a fashionable dark glow.

Packed in membranes, such grease was so highly prized that it was often used as a gift when a favor was desired. Jokingly perhaps at first, a fellow who wished a concession from an official would offer him a gift of "grease for his palm." This usually took the form of gold or silver, so by the sixteenth century to *grease one's palm* was commonly used to designate bribery.

Feeling One's Oats

AMERICAN frontiersmen found natural grasses so abundant that few of them bothered to sow grain. Only race horses and the favorite mounts of landed aristocrats were stall-fed. Naturally, high mettle was a characteristic of blooded animals that had good food, plenty of exercise, and little hard work. Many horsemen ignored other factors and attributed such spirits to diet. Thus in 1843, the Canadian humorist Thomas Haliburton used the expression *feeling one's oats* to mean full of pep and high spirits and showing off.

Peg Out

DEVOTEES of cribbage are eager to *peg out*, or win a bout. This expression for finishing a game proved so apt that it entered common speech as an indication for finishing the most important game of all. As early as 1850 a person who died was likely to be described as having pegged out.

Slipshod

LIGHT house slippers of various design became popular in the 1400s. Made without heels or fastening devices, they were easy to slip on and off the foot. Thin felt was the usual material used in making them. Such slip-shoes, as they were called, were designed for indoor use, but careless persons sometimes wore them when strolling near the house, or even on longer excursions. By 1580 it was proverbial that a shameless person would go slip-shod even to church. Such an individual was likely to be slovenly in his or her entire dress, so a man or woman careless in any respect was dubbed *slipshod*.

Cajole

NOISY and quarrelsome, the jay is among the most common birds of Europe. Though not colored so vividly as the American blue jay, most species have a few blue-and-black striped feathers. Individual specimens sometimes have remarkable ability to imitate sounds made by humans. Consequently, some medieval French sportsmen prized the jay as a household pet.

Such a bird was often kept in a cage, just as canaries are kept by modern householders. Unlike the canary, the jay has a harsh and guttural voice. When a bird is in good health, he will screech for food until his owner gives him all he can eat. His cry is unlike other common sounds, so a special name became attached to it. Imitating his noise, *cajole* came to stand for the chatter of a caged jay. Eventually the odd word was applied to those who wheedle, whine, or beg in order to get what they want.

Guttersnipe

THE snipe was one of the most prized game birds of medieval England, and it was prevalent in swamps and marshes as well as along the banks of small streams. In those days a brook was known as a gutter, so the bird was referred to as the guttersnipe.

This bird was constantly picking in mud and scum in search of food. Beggars had the same habit—getting their food by picking up scraps from the streets. Therefore a human who lived from the gutters of a city came to be called a *guttersnipe*. Soon the word was being applied to a street urchin or a person of the lowest class.

Hail Fellow Well Met

ONE of the longest phrases used as a single word in our language is *hail fellow well met*. Applied to jovial persons, the expression comes from the Anglo-Saxon greeting *hal* ("may you be in good health") that evolved into the convivial "wassail" bowl popular at Christmas. As early as the sixteenth century, men were greeting each other, "Hail, fellow! Well met," in the same jocular spirit that sometimes prompts a modern friend to ask, "What's cooking?" Around 1850 the phrase began to be used as though it were a single descriptive word for a convivial person.

CHAPTER 10

TRANSPORTATION AND TRAVEL

MAKE BOTH ENDS MEET

STARBOARD /
   LARBOARD / PORT

SAIL UNDER FALSE COLORS

AT LOOSE ENDS

IN THE DOGHOUSE

ALL AT SEA

BARGE IN

CRUISE

CONDUCTOR

CHASSIS

TRAIN

TUNNEL

PASSENGER

AMBULANCE

LOCOMOTIVE / CAR

CARBURETOR

MAIL

Make Both Ends Meet

SAILING vessels of the 1500s and 1600s became amazingly complex. Some of the larger ships had a number of masts and a very elaborate system of sails. Since each canvas was raised and lowered separately, rigging involved hundreds of ropes. Many of the lifting ropes, or halyards, were movable and were easy to repair when they broke.

Some ropes were permanently fixed, however. The lower edges of certain sails were held down by tacks and sheets, one end of which was tied to the deck and the other to the canvas. When such a rope broke, most masters preferred to replace it rather than attempt a repair job.

Owners were frugal, however, and a shipper might instruct his captain to pull broken rope ends together and splice them. In order to make both ends of a fixed rope meet, it was often necessary to stretch a piece of rigging to the limit.

From this literal meaning, *make both ends meet* left the sea and entered common speech to stand for living within one's income, however meager.

Starboard / Larboard / Port

ON the surface there seems no good reason why the sides of a ship should be called starboard and port. When first used, however, the terms were sensible enough. Saxon sailing vessels were steered by a big board or oar that protruded from the right side. Hence, in Old English that side of a ship was called *steorboard* ("steer board").

In order to get next to a dock, a vessel had to turn its rudder to the outside. So the left side, invariably used for loading, was called the *lurebord* ("empty side") as the steerman and the steering mechanism were on the other side. Modified into *starboard* and *larboard*, the terms were standard for centuries.

These words sounded so much alike that they were confused.

Since the larboard side was always next to the dock when the ship entered a harbor, *port* came to be substituted for it.

Sail under False Colors

FEW centuries have seen ocean rivalry so keen as during the 1600s. Spain, Portugal, England, and Holland were bidding for supremacy. Treasure discovered in the New World was brought home in such quantity that a single vessel might be loaded with cargo worth many thousands of pounds.

Under these conditions piracy flourished. Many sea robbers were independents, or freebooters. Others held commissions from one or another European ruler. There was little difference between the privateer and the pirate except that the former did not prey on shipping of his own nation.

According to the law of the sea, every ship was supposed to display a flag or color. This showed its national origin and identified it as a potential friend or enemy. Many a pirate and privateer made it his practice to sail under false colors. That is, he displayed the flag of some nation other than his own. Using this device to get close to a ship he wished to capture, he would wait until very near it to raise his true colors and at the same instant he would fire a broadside.

Today's travelers aren't likely to be hijacked on the open seas, but to *sail under false colors* is a derogatory term for those who pretend to be what they are not.

At Loose Ends

DURING days of the windjammers and other great sailing vessels, rigging grew more and more complex. On many ships there were literally hundreds of ropes. If these ropes had been left free to ravel, a hopeless tangle would have resulted. So every ship's master prided himself on the good condition of his "ends"—the taped ends of his ropes.

When other work was slack, members of the crew were frequently put to work repairing the loose ends. Many a captain was accused of ordering such work to keep his men occupied, so a person with nothing important to do is said to be *at loose ends.*

In the Doghouse

COUPLES who keep each other *in the doghouse* may not know it, but the expression goes back to the days of the African slave trade.

Profits in the evil business were great, but so was the danger. In addition to the hazards of crossing the Atlantic in sailing vessels, the slave trader was constantly menaced by the possibility that his "cargo" would break their chains and kill their captors. Therefore, many Yankee sailors slept on deck, after closing and locking the hatches at night.

Some sort of shelter was necessary, so many sailors covered the poop deck of the ship with tiny sleeping cubicles. Their small size suggested a doghouse. Though officers frequently had to sleep in them, they were so uncomfortable that *in the doghouse* came to indicate any state of discomfort—physical or mental.

All at Sea

NO feeling of helplessness is more complete than that of being lost at sea. Crude compasses were in use as early as 1250, but the instruments were clumsy and inaccurate. Small vessels made a practice to try to keep within sight of land. Sometimes a "coast hugger" was blown off course or sailed far out to sea. If the captain lost his bearings on such an occasion, the ship was in for trouble. When hurricanes ripped through the sails of larger vessels, they were helpless regardless of their size. With nothing visible but water, the crew of a ship whose position was not known was literally *all at sea.* Borrowed from navigators, the expression came into general use to indicate any state of helplessness or bewilderment.

Barge In

EUROPEANS who participated in the Crusades brought home many devices and words from their extensive travels. Seamen were especially impressed by a small sailing vessel used on the Nile by Egyptians. From the Latin word *barca,* the word passed through Old French into Middle English to become *barge.*

These boats were designed with flat bottoms in order to sail in shallow water, proving useful in canals as well as rivers. They were generally pulled by animals on the bank and were hard to steer. Accidents were frequent, for once a barge got under way, it was difficult to stop it or alter its course. They often bumped into other boats.

By the nineteenth century English schoolboys were using the term *barge about* to describe hustling a person by bumping or pushing him around. In the early 1900s *barge in* came to mean to butt in, not a physical activity but just as annoying.

Cruise

FRENCH, English, and Dutch privateers roamed the seas in the sixteenth, seventeenth, and eighteenth centuries preying on shipping. Such freebooters didn't sail according to a definite schedule but crossed back and forth along shipping lanes in search of victims. This zigzag movement came to be called *kruisen,* the Dutch word for "cross." The English borrowed the word and modified it to "cruise." For several generations the term was reserved for such crisscross sailing as that of a warship seeking an enemy vessel.

Then owners of pleasure boats began to use the word to stand for any trip not held to a schedule. By the time steamers made tourist travel cheap and popular, almost any type of pleasure voyage was being called a *cruise.* During the twentieth century, abundance of money and time fostered the rise of luxury liners especially designed for vacationers, and cruise ships proliferated.

Conductor

MILITARY expeditions were the largest transportation proj-
ects of medieval Europe. There was little progress toward central-
ized management, however. Every group of fighting men hauled
what it needed in heavy wagons—drawn sometimes by horses and
sometimes by oxen. The driver came to be called the conductor
(from the Latin *con*, "with," and *ducere*, "to lead"). As more complex organization developed, his title passed to the official who
directed an entire wagon train.

Eventually it became standard practice to send a conductor with
every stagecoach. He had authority over the vehicle with special
responsibility for meeting the schedule, handling passengers, baggage, and mail. Frequently he was a veteran driver or guard whose
service record won him a promotion.

With the advent of railroads, their workers adopted many
occupational names current among stage-line workers, and by
1830 it was customary to place every train under the supervision
of a trained *conductor*. With the demise of most U.S. passenger
trains, the old vocational term is now used most often in connection with the person who leads members of an orchestra or band.

Chassis

ROMANS of the late Empire commonly referred to a closed place
as a *chas*. Their word was borrowed by tribesmen of northern Europe
and eventually entered modern French as *châssis*, meaning "frame."
Ordinary usage gradually restricted the word's meaning, so that it
came to stand for the wooden frame enclosing an opening in a house.

Wealthy English people borrowed the idea, and by the sixteenth
century many a mansion boasted a wall with at least one chassis
holding oiled paper to admit light. Glass later replaced paper in the
household chassis, but the word did not disappear. Instead, it transferred to the base frame of a casemate gun developed about 1850.
Since the gun base was not unlike a common window frame, the
transition was natural.

Fifty years later, pioneer automobile makers found it desirable to employ frames similar to those of artillery carriages. As a result, today's cars and trucks are mounted on a chassis that's at least a trifle like an old artillery carriage whose name was borrowed from architecture.

Train

NORMAN warriors who invaded England under William the Conqueror in A.D. 1066 mastered the island in spite of transportation difficulties. They were unable to bring with them enough wagons to haul all their gear, so they cut trees and improvised crude sleds. Loaded with supplies, these cumbersome vehicles followed the victorious troops, who called anything dragged a *train*, from their word *trainer* ("to drag or draw").

Wagon trains abound in novels of the Wild West and followed Union and Rebel armies during the Civil War. In the mid-nineteenth century locomotives began to pull railway carriages behind them, just as horses had pulled trains. Thus *train* took on an entirely new meaning.

Another old meaning also survives. Brides still walk down the aisle "draggin" a train behind them.

Tunnel

NORMAN artisans of the late Middle Ages achieved great skill in making barrels and casks. They referred to such a container as a "tonel," and applied its name to barrel-shaped passages sometimes cut in hills by underground streams.

English who adopted this usage modified the spelling to

"tunnel," but no important work was done in building tunnels until late in the 1700s. Practically all early tunnels were made by enlarging natural openings. In several instances, earth and rock were hewn out above streams that flowed under mountains. One such passage, enlarged for towing coal barges, twisted and turned for two miles.

Sweeping changes in bulk transportation elevated man-made tunnels into great significance. From the first decade that a wholly artificial *tunnel* was in use, it was apparent that the iron horse could move goods faster and cheaper than any other device then in existence. Huge amounts could be spent on engineering, yet overall savings could result.

Tunnel building became a specialized skill, and railroads were soon using underground passages that did not remotely resemble wine barrels from which their name came. Only a small fraction of today's travelers ever rides through a railroad tunnel, but the "tunnel of love" found in some theme parks preserves the specialized term.

Passenger

DURING the Crusades thousands of people traveled through Europe on their way to the Holy Lands. Such a traveler was called a *passager*, a Middle French word for "one who passes" from the Old French word *passer*, meaning "to pass." The expression was brought to England by returning Crusaders and became *passenger*.

Fare-paying passengers were common on stage lines, but it took the iron horse to give the old word real vitality. Locomotives may have pulled passenger cars as early as 1833. It was not until much later, however, that riders became abundant enough to warrant special trains which—from their cargo—were called passengers.

In the twenty-first century the vast majority of the world's passengers go to and fro by way of subways, elevated railways leading into cities, and airplanes that make thousands of flights every day.

Ambulance

NO army had anything comparable to a modern medical corps until the eighteenth century. France led the way by adopting a first-aid wagon that moved behind battle lines with a stock of medicines and bandages. Such a vehicle was termed a *hôpital ambulant* ("moving hospital"). Borrowed by the English, the term was altered to *ambulance*.

During the Crimean War, battlefield first aid proved inadequate—it was necessary to remove serious cases to hospitals behind the lines. For this purpose it was logical to use an ambulance, which quickly became the standard vehicle for transporting sick and wounded civilians as well as soldiers.

Locomotive / Car

IN 1627 an English physician described a patient as having "no locomotive faculty, no power to stiree hand or foote." His word for the power of movement derived from the Latin *loco* ("place") and *motivus* ("moving").

A lengthy name of a discovery or invention is often abbreviated in common speech. That was the case with the "locomotive steam engine." As soon as the engine began to be talked about regularly, people began clipping off part of the name. By 1829 members of the board of directors of the Liverpool and Manchester Railroad issued a statement in which they listed "locomotives" owned by the company.

Still used to describe any self-moving steam-powered vehicle, *locomotive* attached exclusively to railroad engines during succeeding decades. This usage led to calling a self-propelled gasoline-driven vehicle an "automobile carriage"—a title that was soon abbreviated to the ever popular *car*.

Carburetor

SCIENTISTS were working on methods to increase the combustion power of carbon and its compounds as early as the eighteenth century. Several gadgets were perfected by which some form of the element could be mixed with liquids or gases. Such a device was called a "carburetor"—a name only slightly altered from "carbon."

By 1850 there were commercial sales of a contrivance which forced illuminating gas through liquid hydrocarbon. This added greatly to the brilliance of light produced.

Greatly modified in form, carbon-mixing devices were used on early gasoline motors. It was natural that such a vaporizer should be termed a *carburetor*, for its function was to mix air and "petroleum essence." By 1896 the name of the carbon mixer had become firmly attached to any type of gasoline vaporizer.

Mail

DURING the 1400s King Edward IV set up a system of royal couriers, which was primarily for carrying official mail. Men and horses were stationed at intervals on a few major roads. When an official message was sent along the route, riders carried the "king's packet" from one point to the next. They soon began taking letters of ordinary citizens and businessmen as well. By 1625 more than a hundred men were engaged in this work. Since messages were relayed from station to station, or post to post, the system came to be known as the "postal service."

Letters were carried in a leather bag or pack, called a "male." As early as 1654 specific postal regulations were devised. They included provisions that directed the rider just how he should carry his "male of letters." This usage led to calling the letters themselves "male." The word was confused so often with the standard term for a person of the male sex that the name of the transported message became *mail*.

CHAPTER 11

GROWING THINGS

CALAMITY

DAISY

DANDELION

FLOWER NAMES

HOLLYHOCK

MARIGOLD

IODINE

GRAIN

DELIRIUM

MARSHMALLOW

HECKLE

Calamity

THOUGH early Greek farmers planted several types of grain, the most important was *calamus*, a kind of wheat. Success of the crop meant prosperity for the region; failure spelled hard times or even famine.

Suffering was almost certain to follow when drought, storms, insects, or mildew damaged the calamus crop. Such a disaster came to be called *calamitas*. Modified only slightly by centuries of use, the word entered English when the British Isles fell to French invaders. By the time of its first literary appearance in 1490, *calamity* had spread from the farm to stand for any type of dire happening.

Daisy

THE ancients, who lived close to nature, were familiar with a flower having a yellow center and white or pink petals that closed its petals and went to sleep at night, only to open its eyes again the next morning. Because of this opening-and-closing action, the plant became known to the Anglo-Saxons as *daeges eage* ("day's eye").

Medieval times saw the spelling changed to "dayeseye," in which the original meaning was still clear. Modernized spelling brought still other modifications. Hence, though the plant still closes its eyes at night and opens them at dawn, the modern word *daisy* gives little indication that the flower got its name from its practice of opening its "eyes" soon after daylight.

Dandelion

EARLY French naturalists who had never seen a lion fancied that leaves of a small plant resembled the shape of teeth belonging to the king of beasts. Accordingly they called the plant *dent de lion* ("lion's tooth"). Though we now know that the resemblance was imaginary, the name *dandelion* perpetuates the error.

Flower Names

TRACED to their sources, the names of many flowers show how keenly they were observed by early growers.

An ancient blossom tormented the nose of those who sniffed it, so the nose twister was called *nasturtium*, from *nasus* ("nose") and *torquea* ("twist"). Centuries later, French gardeners noticed that the expanded blossom of a little flower resembled a *tulipan* ("turban"), so they named it *tulip*. Still later Linnaeus—a noted botanist—observed that the seed capsule of a familiar flower is shaped like a cup or miniature water pitcher. Delving into Greek, he combined *hydor* ("water") and *angos* ("vessel") to coin the name *hydrangea*.

Hollyhock

BEFORE A.D. 1000, pilgrimages were being made to the Isle of Farne, off the northeast coast of England, where Saint Cuthbert had lived in the seventh century.

Visitors to the sacred spot discovered a native plant growing in profusion, which they called "Saint Cuthbert's cole." A kind of *hock*, as the plant we call mallow was then known, it grew in marshes and swamps.

By the sixteenth century the plant associated with the saint was widely known as *holi hocke* ("holy mallow"). Later generations slurred the name to *hollyhock*, the same way they slurred holy day into holiday.

Marigold

DURING one of the early Crusades, Christian warriors discovered a striking little yellow flower. They took some of its roots back to Europe, and in honor of the holy Virgin, the mother of Christ, they reverently called the plant "Mary's gold."

It was used as a poultice for wounds and also as a flavor for soups and stews. Slurred over in common speech, the name of the flower was abbreviated to *marigold*.

Iodine

JOSEPH Louis Gay-Lussac, most noted French chemist of his generation, was the natural person to consult about any odd substance. One of his fellow scientists, while experimenting with ashes from burnt seaweed, isolated a strange grayish-black solid. He had no idea what it might be or whether it would prove of any use so he sent a specimen to the Sorbonne.

Gay-Lussac studied the queer stuff and concluded it to be a new element. At ordinary temperatures he found the substance to behave in staid fashion, but when he heated a quantity to 185 degrees, it changed to a strange blue-violet vapor. There was a striking resemblance between the color of the odd gas and that of the chemist's favorite flower—the violet.

It was customary to base scientific names upon Greek words. So the Frenchman took "iode," the classical name for the common violet, and modified it to designate the strange new substance. Experimenting with iode, Sir Humphrey Davy found it to have many valuable properties. Its flower-based name was modified to *iodine* and the new chemical became a standard weapon in the war against bacteria.

Grain

JEWELERS and dealers in rare metals have always faced special difficulties in weighing their goods. Large units are not satisfactory for measuring valuables, and until modern times it was difficult to secure small units of uniform size.

English lawmakers of the seventeenth century met the problem by adopting a new standard of weight. After much searching they decided that grains of wheat are the most nearly identical of tiny natural objects. So a grain was established as the legal unit for weighing gold, spices, and other valuables.

Recognizing the possibility of variation even within a wheat field, it was stipulated that grains used for weighing should be "drie, and gathered from the middle of the eare."

Today *grain* is the smallest unit in the avoirdupois system of weights. It equals 0.0648 grams. The name is also used for one-fourth of a carat.

Delirium

EARLY Roman farmers took great pride in the appearance of their land. It was considered especially important that the *lira*, or ridges made in plowing, be both straight and regular.

A careless husbandman who made balks and irregular furrows was said to *delirare*. Hence, anyone whose mental faculties were like a field full of irregularities was termed *delirus*. Slight changes in spelling produced the familiar word *delirium*, which on the surface shows no connection with growing things.

Marshmallow

ONE of the most common plants of medieval England was the mallow. It was abundant in many varieties; some hardy forms even grew among salt marshes. Long regarded as a weed, this marsh mallow suddenly burst into prominence when herb fanciers learned to make a potent medicine from its roots.

Syrup from the marsh mallow proved an effective remedy for coughs. Mothers experimented on their children and gradually came to regard the herb as a cure-all. According to a medical book published in 1680, the syrup was the sovereign remedy for half a hundred illnesses.

Someone later discovered that a novel confection resulted from mixing gum arabic with syrup of the marsh mallow. It proved so popular that a substitute was developed from gelatin and sugar. Though not even remotely connected with herbs from England's marshes, the modern delicacy has taken over the name *marshmallow*.

Heckle

FLAX was the chief vegetable fiber used in medieval cloth making. Though its fibers are long and strong, their preparation presented many problems to the prescientific age. Stalks were first permitted to putrefy; then they were split and combed by hand with a brush with iron teeth. The instrument was known as a heckle, from an Anglo-Saxon term *hecel* ("to split"). By the fifteenth century the word was in use as a verb meaning "to scratch with a steel brush," or to look for weak points.

Scottish candidates for public office were customarily subjected to public questioning. Voters were merciless in looking for weak points in those whom they opposed. So *heckle* was borrowed from the flax floor and applied to any disturbance intended to distract a public speaker.

CHAPTER 12

COMMON SPEECH

ALLERGY

GOLDBRICK

PUT ON THE DOG

NAIL A LIE TO
   THE COUNTER

CASE

HOBO/STREET PEOPLE

GARBLE

SEASONING

PIGGY BANK

GET UP ON THE WRONG
   SIDE OF THE BED

TOO MANY IRONS
   IN THE FIRE

SIDEKICK

DYED IN THE WOOL

GET DOWN TO BRASS TACKS

THINKING CAP

ALL WOOL AND A
   YARD WIDE

BUTTONHOLE

THREADBARE

OUTSKIRTS

CLOTH NAMES FROM
   FRANCE

CLOTH NAMES FROM
   CHINA

CLOTH NAMES FROM
   INDIA

CLOTH NAMES FROM
   BRITISH PLACES

CLOTH NAMES FROM
   THE NEAR EAST

GRIT

BLACK SHEEP

WINDFALL

CAP

CAMERA

THROW COLD WATER

KNOW LIKE A BOOK

Allergy

LATE in the nineteenth century, physicians developed great interest in a puzzling phenomenon. Patients who were helped by the first dose of a new drug sometimes had adverse reactions to later doses. At loss for a more precise name, specialists used the Greek word *allos* ("other") to coin the word *allergy*, a condition in which reactions are other than standard.

By 1925 the new word had come into general use to name a variety of peculiar phenomena of altered reactivity. Since then the proliferation of new drugs makes it strange if an individual doesn't show at least one "other than expected" reaction to some food, drug, or natural substance.

Goldbrick

IN the western mining communities in the nineteenth century, everyone was eager to get rich, and great fortunes were often being dug out of the ground. Sharpers frequently covered iron bricks with a thin layer of gold. It was not hard to persuade a greedy but gullible investor to grab a big profit for himself by buying a gold brick at a "give-away" price. There's a record of $3,700 having been paid for one of them. This game worked so well so often that *goldbrick* entered common speech as a synonym for "swindle." In World War I soldiers picked up the expression and began using it to mean shirking one's duties or responsibilities. Today's scam artists may not hawk "gold" bricks, but they go in for pyramid schemes, sweepstakes, and e-mail rip-offs that are a lot more elaborate but produce the same end results to the credulous.

Put on the Dog

FEW decades in American history have
been so colorful as the ones between the
Civil War and the end of the century. It
was a generation of easy money. Many
manufacturers had grown wealthy during the war, and bold spirits won
quick fortunes through railroads, oil,
or real estate.

While many of the newly rich
had as much money as the old aristocracy, they lacked the same culture. Hence they found it hard to
win social acceptance. To make
up for this, many of the newly
rich were wildly extravagant.

Lap dogs, perennially popular
in Europe, became all the rage
among the wives of American millionaires. They spent fantastic sums on their pets, and each tried to top the excesses of the
other. Cynical observers began to identify pampered poodles with
the desire for show. So people who made a flashy display were
said to *put on the dog*. Firmly fixed in language by 1885, the
phrase was soon used to label pretentiousness of every sort.

Nail a Lie to the Counter

WHEN a person becomes righteously indignant about some
untruth that is circulating, he may threaten to nail it to the counter.
This vivid expression for exposure of anything false resulted from
an unusual practice among American merchants.

During the early 1800s bad money was more abundant than at
any time before or since. There were so many types of bogus currency in circulation that in 1826 a publisher found it profitable to
issue *Day's New York Bank Note List and Counterfeit Detector*.

Frontier shopkeepers adopted a no-nonsense approach to the problem. When a merchant was given a coin that he recognized as bogus, he took a hammer and nailed it to his counter. This served a double purpose: he could compare doubtful coins with specimens in his collection, and would-be sharpers were warned not to attempt to pass bad money in his store.

So many phony coins were displayed by merchants who detected them that to *nail a lie to the counter* came into general use to expose something false or bogus.

Case

MANY card games—of which faro is a notable example— have flourished for a period, only to fall into disfavor. Now familiar only to patrons of swank gambling houses, faro was once the rage of the American frontier.

As played in the West, the game featured a case, or frame, on which each card was placed after it was played. Big games employed a special case keeper who did nothing but arrange dead cards for display. It was essential for each player to quickly case, or examine, the displayed cards in order to make best use of those he held.

This practice was so familiar that a person who studied any situation as cautiously as though it were a faro case was said to case the place. After faro began losing ground to poker, the slang associated with the old game gradually lost its meaning for most people. Among criminals, however, it became standard practice to *case* the joint before starting a robbery or other crime.

Hobo / Street People

AFTER the Civil War bands of migratory farm laborers became familiar in many states. They had no homes and each year followed the crops to find work. Farm machinery was limited in use, and most operations involved hand labor with a hoe.

Consequently, the wandering workman was known as a "hoe boy." Many of these hoe boys were not above petty theft, and the term became one of reproach. By 1891 the modified name *hobo* was applied to knights of the road who prided themselves on never doing a day's work with a hoe or anything else.

Wandering hoboes have virtually disappeared, with their place taken by comparatively sedentary *street people* whose name stems from the fact that they live on the streets of cities and towns.

Garble

ONLY a few substances that can be used to flavor foods are native to Europe. By the 1200s, spices were being imported from the Far East, and one of the chief centers of the trade was Alexandria, where cargoes were unloaded for resale to western Europe. After the long journey by caravan across Asia, wholesale merchants had to go through each lot of spices to separate the good from the bad. In Arabic this operation was called *gharbala* ("to sift").

Then, no matter how carefully the sifting was done, sea water, mildew, and rot caused additional damage by the time the cargo reached Britain, where the process came to be known as "garble."

By 1650 the term invaded the literary world. Persons were said to *garble* a religious or political paper when they selectively sifted out words to distort meaning. Obviously, such a procedure frequently muddled the meaning of the writer, so today the word means mixed-up or incomprehensible.

Seasoning

ROMAN farmers had a special word for "sowing time," which passed into Old French as *seison*. In that form, it stood for any indefinite period of time.

Housewives knew that certain foods improved by being aged.

Wines, cheeses, and some kinds of meat became more tasty after a long or short season of time. The process of aging came to be known as *saisonner*.

Carried to England by her invaders from the Continent, the expression became "season." Since it made food more palatable to season it, the word attached to the use of salt, sugar, herbs, and spices in cooking. By the fourteenth century any type of spice or condiment was being called *seasoning*.

Piggy Bank

A FIFTEENTH-CENTURY pot or jar made from one kind of clay was called a *pygg*, from an obscure word for the clay. Evidently this raw material was abundant, for its name eventually attached to all earthenware.

Then as now, frugal housewives frequently dropped their coins into a pygg for safekeeping. Perhaps influenced by the old name of the earthenware container, potters of the 1800s began making pig-shaped coin holders for children. This practice caught the public fancy so effectively that it became customary to call a coin box a *piggy bank*, no matter what its shape or composition.

Get Up on the Wrong Side of the Bed

FEW superstitions have been more widely held than those concerning the sinister nature of the left side. The Latin word *sinister* meant "on the left" or "unlucky." In Rome a left-handed person was considered to be a bearer of bad luck. Any act involving the left was often regarded with suspicion and dread. For example, a wise person made it a habit to get out of bed on the right side. If he occasionally crawled out on the left side, bad luck was believed to almost certainly follow.

A person expecting to encounter trouble is seldom in the best of moods, so irritability came to be associated with getting out of bed on the left, or wrong side. This notion was so widely accepted that when we encounter ill-natured people, we still say that it looks as though they *got up on the wrong side of the bed.*

Too Many Irons in the Fire

MODERN householders who take the electric iron for granted do not always realize what a boon it actu- ally is. Until electricity became available, it was necessary to heat an iron by placing it among the glowing embers of a fire or in the eye of a wood-burning stove.

The irons stayed hot only a short time, so it was customary to use several—ironing with one while the others were heat- ing. It required no small amount of skill to keep the irons at the right temperature.

An amateur who tried to speed up work by using five or six flatirons usually discovered that it was difficult or impossible to keep up with all of them. If an iron remained on the heat too long, it became so hot that it scorched the garment on which it was used. A common tendency to have *too many irons in the fire* resulted in application of the expression to the broader sense of being involved simultaneously in too many activities.

Sidekick

FEW criminal groups of modern times have enjoyed such a field day as did English pickpockets of the 1700s. They organized guilds, and recruits had to go through an apprenticeship. They also worked in America, and, as all criminals do, they developed a spe- cial vocabulary for their trade.

They called a hip pocket a "pratt" and a breast pocket a "pit." A vest pocket was known as a "jerve," and a side pocket of trousers was called a "kick." No matter how nimble the fingers of a pickpocket, he usually had trouble with a kick, since it lay close to the victim's hand and was constantly moving with the legs. Therefore, if a man wanted to keep his wallet, he was wise to put it in his side kick. Later *sidekick* came to stand for a faithful partner who, like a trouser pocket, is always at one's side.

Dyed in the Wool

ANY Technicolor movies set in the Middle Ages that show the characters in a variety of brightly colored costumes are lacking historical accuracy, for modern chemical dyes date from the 1700s. In earlier periods even members of royalty wore comparatively drab clothing.

With few exceptions, dyes were of vegetable origin, and they seldom retained their brilliance through many washings. This was especially true of woolen clothing, which was likely to be blotched and uneven at the moment it was taken from the dye vat.

Some artisan made a revolutionary discovery that led to dyeing raw wool instead of garments or bolts of cloth. Colors were much more firmly fixed than earlier, and fabric made of dyed wool had a uniform appearance. As a result it became customary to praise such goods as *dyed in the wool,* and in time the phrase came to stand for high quality in general.

Get Down to Brass Tacks

JUST why getting down to brass tacks should mean abandoning the preliminaries and getting down to business, no one knows positively. The only plausible explanation traces the expression to early dry-goods stores.

Piece goods were sold by the yard, and merchants found it convenient to put tacks in the edge of the counter to indicate a yard, half-yard, and quarter-yard. Only brass-headed tacks resisted rust and remained clearly visible.

Since the practice of putting price tags on merchandise had not been introduced, the frugal purchaser inquired the price of an article. If the price were considered too high, a period of haggling was likely to follow. Once that came to an end, the merchant might say, "All right; now let's get down to brass tacks and measure the cloth."

Intense and prolonged dickering made no sales. Only when cloth went down on the counter alongside the brass-headed tacks that measured it was any business actually transacted.

Thinking Cap

SCHOLARS in the Middle Ages wore a distinctive costume. Some of its details varied from one university to another, but two basic pieces were standard—a long black gown and a square-cut cap that fitted tightly against the skull. Clergymen and jurists also wore gowns, so the odd little cap became the symbol of the professional scholar.

Most common folk of the era were illiterate. They had great respect for any man who wore the cap that showed him to possess learning. There was a widespread notion that the cap actually aided its owner to think. Many an idle fellow boasted about what he would do if only he could get a *thinking cap*.

This superstition disappeared long ago. So did the "thinking cap," though it left its mark on academic headgear of the third millennium. The expression linked to the costume of early scholars remains in speech, so those wishing to analyze a problem are likely to say that they must put on their *thinking cap* even if they remain bare headed.

All Wool and a Yard Wide

UNTIL very recent times there were few regulations governing the quality of consumer goods. Manufacturers and merchants operated on the principle "Let the buyer beware." Standards varied widely, both in terms of quality and quantity.

This was particularly true of the textile trade, in which it was easy for a manufacturer to mix mohair or mill waste with wool and sell the product as first quality. At the same time he might reduce the width of his cloth to thirty-five or even thirty-four inches.

Around 1850 English textile makers began a reform movement. They produced cloth which they guaranteed to be free of fillers and woven full measure. As a result *all wool and a yard wide* entered common speech as a synonym for "genuine."

Buttonhole

IN the early nineteenth century, men's coats could be buttoned all the way up to the neck. Except in extreme weather, however, it was customary to leave the coat open at the throat. The unused buttons proved a great advantage to gossips and businessmen alike. A man with a yarn to spin or goods to sell would stop to talk with a victim. In order to prevent a hurried escape, the talker would seize a button and hold it. Thus the term "buttonhold" came into existence.

When fashion decreed a change in the design of men's coats, both of the upper front edges were folded back to form lapels, and the upper buttons were eliminated.

No longer having a top button to grasp, an eager talker often took hold of his victim's lapel. Since "buttonhold" sounds so much like "buttonhole," by 1860 *buttonhol*e was being used to name the act of forcing attention upon a reluctant listener.

Threadbare

ARTISANS of medieval Europe developed great skill in the manufacture of textiles. Among their innovations were new methods for spinning strands with short fibers, which were smoothed and cut after weaving was completed. This process yielded a rich nap on such textiles as fine velvets.

It was not unusual for a miserly or impoverished nobleman to wear a once-splendid garment until its nap was worn off in many places. In such condition bare threads of warp and woof were clearly visible. Associates frequently jeered at the wearer of *threadbare* finery, and the colorful word attached to all well-worn clothing. Geoffrey Chaucer helped fix the term in speech by referring to a "threadbare cape" in one of his Canterbury tales. The old textile term has survived all subsequent changes in cloth production and applies to wearing shabby or worn-out clothing.

Outskirts

Radical changes in every area of English life resulted from the conquest of the island by William the Conqueror. Norman ladies turned up their noses at simple Anglo-Saxon clothing and wore an elaborate outer garment which they called a "skirt."

Soon it was observed that a fringe of houses clustered outside town walls was much like a skirt surrounding a woman's feet. So it became customary to speak of a city's edge as its "skirts." Naturally, one who wished to indicate a house or inn lying at the extreme outer border of a community described it as being in the *outskirts*.

Cloth Names from France

French cities have given their names to many fabrics. Manufactured in Cambrai, a type of fine white linen came to be in great demand before Columbus made his first voyage to the New World. Strictly a luxury item, Cambrai linen soon had its name abbreviated to modern *cambric*.

Laon, a city northwest of Reims specializing in sheer linen that was used chiefly in making sleeves of ecclesiastical garments, had its name transformed into *lawn*. In the south of France, citizens of Nîmes specialized in a kind of serge that was marketed as *serge de Nîmes*. It was an easy transition to *denim*, now worn around the world.

A heavy unglazed cotton fabric, often used for draperies and made in Creton became *cretonne*. At least one French fabric was naturalized in Great Britain without a change in name. A soft, fine, net-like material made in Tulle in southwest France is still called *tulle*.

Cloth Names from China

EUROPEANS made occasional contact with China very early in the first millennium, but nothing like organized commerce took place until modern times. Beginning in the 1600s, trade with what was then called Cathay reached significant proportions. One of the most important articles of the trade between the Chinese and Europeans was cloth, which was imported in large quantities. Some of the native names cling to fabrics now mass-produced in today's western world.

Nankeen is a slightly-modified spelling of Nanking, the ancient capital of southern China. Cotton grown in that district had a natural yellow color and was made into dainty fabric. *Shantung* originally came from the province of Shantung, or Shandong ("Eastern Mountains"), in which Confucius was born and reared. Here wild silkworms fed on oak leaves are used to produce the fabric that corresponded roughly with European homespun. Because it included frequent irregularities, this fabric was called *ben ji* ("own loom"). Exported first as "paunchee," it later came to be called *pongee*.

Cloth Names from India

DUNGAREE was first made in quantity in the Dungri suburb of Bombay. Coarse and durable, it was fashioned into sails and heavy sheets. At about the middle of the nineteenth century, an English manufacturer dyed a batch of this cloth blue and made it into trousers that took the name of the fabric and were widely worn for decades. Today *jeans* or *Levi's* are used more frequently than *dungarees* for pants made from the coarse cloth.

Hindustani *chint* ("spotted cloth") survives in *chintz*. *Gingham* is readily seen to be an anglicized variant of Malay's *gingan* ("striped cotton"). One of the most beautiful fabrics imported from the East, *nainsook*, gained its name from Hindustani *nain* ("eye") plus *sukh* ("pleasure").

Also of Hindustani origin, *khaki* is derived from *khak* ("dust"), and originally referred to the color of the Indian material. Khaki was worn by the famous Guides Corps before the mutiny of 1857 and was later adopted for uniforms of all British troops. Today *khaki* refers both to the color (light olive brown to light yellowish brown) and also to soldiers' warm-weather uniforms of this color.

Cloth Names from British Places

GREAT Britain was, for a considerable period, the world's largest manufacturer of cloth.

Three fabrics that became important in international trade took their names from places in which their production was first centered.

Worsted perpetuates Worstead, a town in Norfolk that was elevated into importance by King Edward III. Eager to improve the quality of English woolens, the monarch brought over a group of Flemish weavers in the fourteenth century. He settled them in Worstead and they produced cloth of such high quality that it gained international fame.

Soft woolens made on Jersey, the largest of the Channel Islands, were long used for making stockings, nightgowns, and breeches from *jersey*. Early in the nineteenth century a tunic of new style that was made of jersey became fashionable. Consequently, the name of the fabric attached to the garment.

Balbriggan was an early product of Balbriggan, Ireland. It was widely sold as a material for making men's hose and brought prosperity to the seaport town where it was made.

Cloth Names from the Near East

THE modern state of Israel's problems with the Gaza Strip are well known. Not so well known is the fact that the fabric *gauze*— a thin fabric of loose open weave used in bandages—was first produced in the ancient city of Gaza.

Fine linen made in and around Damascus gave birth to modern *damask*. *Muslin* originated in Mosul, near the ruins of ancient Nineveh in western Mesopotamia. Other fabrics took their names from special qualities. Persian *taftan* ("to shine") gave rise to *taffeta*. Another Persian term, used to indicate "milk and sugar" was called *shirushakar* by Europeans who soon modified the name of the blue-and-white striped linen to *seersucker.*

Grit

DURING the fourth and fifth centuries, fierce Germanic tribes from northern Europe invaded and mastered Britain. Their word *greot* came with them as a designation for sand or crushed stone.

When these people adopted the practice of raising poultry, they discovered that sand or small gravel is essential to the health of birds. Long usage gradually standardized the name of the small hard particles to "grit."

Grit also came to be applied to the coarse, hard sandstone used for making grindstones and millstones. The operation of grinding makes an abrasive sound like when a person "grits one's teeth."

Black Sheep

EFFICIENT methods of processing wool are quite modern. As late as the 1700s, cleaning fibers shorn from sheep was a major operation, and dyeing was even more difficult. Only a few satisfactory dyestuffs were known, and those were expensive. In this situation, ordinary folk used vast quantities of undyed fleece.

Under these conditions off-color wool was low in value. Black sheep were rare, and unless a man owned many flocks he was not likely to produce enough black fleece to market it. Except for mutton, a dark-haired animal was practically worthless to the small farmer. Generations of herdsmen berated the *black sheep* with such vigor that its name attached to any scamp or renegade.

Windfall

ONE of the most vexatious problems of the medieval English household was the shortage of fuel. Trees were not scarce; on the contrary, forests were thick and abundant. But long-standing royal proclamations made it illegal for commoners to fell a tree without permission. Only dead branches and trees blown down by a storm could be used for firewood.

Consequently, the discovery of a fallen tree was a stroke of great good luck. Such a *windfall*, as it was called, might mean the difference between having a warm blaze and going fireless on cold days. From trees felled by the wind, the expression came to be applied to any piece of good fortune.

Cap

ALTHOUGH Latin is now termed a "classical" tongue, when it was spoken by the Romans it included quite a bit of slang. Among the expressions used in informal talk was *capitulare* — a nickname for "headdress" — based upon a term for "head."

This piece of apparel was originally a type of mantle with an attached hood that Roman legionnaires took with them when they followed Caesar to Britain in the first century. Natives adopted the headdress, modified the name, and within a few generations the *caeppe* was frequently seen there.

By the time Chaucer wrote his *Canterbury Tales*, the garment's name was commonly abbreviated to *cap* and was being used chiefly to designate a detachable hood. Its name is now attached to a variety of coverings, from a soft headdress like a baseball cap, to an academic mortarboard, to the fitted covering for a bottle.

Camera

WHEN the Romans invented the arched vault, they called it a *camera*, from a Greek term for "curved." Popular usage eventually made the term stand for any type of chamber even if all of its walls were straight.

With that meaning in mind, English scientists of the 1500s borrowed the old Latin word. They had discovered that a convex lens fixed in one end of a darkened room could be made to throw the image of an external object on the opposite wall. They knew of no practical use for such a dark chamber, but they gave it the Latin name *camera obscura*.

Eventually, a miniature camera obscura was devised. Small enough to be carried from place to place, it was a sealed box with a lens in one end and a view hole in the top. Artists used it in sketching, but no one had any idea that the little "dark chamber" would ever have commercial importance.

Around 1800 Thomas Wedgwood had an inspiration. It was known that light rays affect silver compounds. Inventors had made many attempts to devise a method of bringing an image to focus upon a layer of metal in such fashion that a picture would be burned into it. Wedgwood decided to place a light-sensitive plate into a camera obscura. His experiments proved that photography was more than an idle dream, and the *camera* entered a new phase of its long history.

Throw Cold Water

EIGHTEENTH-CENTURY doctors attributed insanity to excessive bodily fluids, or "humors." Excitability and nervous tension were associated with this condition, so the object of treatment was to reduce the patient's "mental heat." One prescription was hydrotherapy during which the supposedly demented were stripped naked and showered with cold water for long periods. Thoroughly chilled, the patients sometimes became temporarily docile; and for a time the procedure received great publicity. As a result to *throw cold water* entered common speech as an indication for any action tending to produce apathy.

Know Like a Book

ON the American frontier books were scarce. Only the Bible and Webster's blue-backed speller attained anything like national circulation. In this situation, available books were used until they literally wore to pieces. Women who had large families frequently taught each child his letters using one of the two or three books in the village. It was inevitable that many mothers should commit these books to memory. So when a housewife was familiar with some matter, she said she "knew it like a book." This usage was so common that to *know like a book* entered standard speech as an expression for complete understanding.

CHAPTER 13

BODIES AND MINDS

ECCENTRIC

BRAKE

THROW INTO STITCHES

FEEL ONE'S PULSE

NOSTRIL

BY THE SKIN OF THE TEETH

HUNCH

MUSCLE

SKELETON

FEET OF CLAY

TONIC

INSULIN

CALF OF THE LEG

GUTS

HAVE ONE'S HEART
  IN THE RIGHT PLACE

Eccentric

MORE than one noted thinker has declared the wheel to be man's most important invention. By the time early Greeks established their city-states, wheels were so much in demand that professional craftsmen manufactured them in large numbers. Their methods were crude, however, so hubs of many wheels were off-center, or *ex kentron*.

Whether on a farmer's cart or a soldier's war chariot, an off-center wheel made for bumpy travel. This problem persisted as European civilization expanded, and it became more acute with the development of better roads. During late medieval times the term changed to *eccentricus*. These wheels gave so much trouble that the name was borrowed to stand for a person who behaved as though off-center. By 1650 the term was shortened, and any person of odd or whimsical habits was dubbed *eccentric*.

Brake

UNTIL comparatively recent times, flax was the most important fiber grown in northern Europe. Easy to produce, it was hard to prepare for cloth making. One phase of this process involved crushing or breaking tough flax stalks. For this purpose Dutch workmen devised a special pronged implement which they called a *brake*.

Teeth of the flax-crusher gave blacksmiths an idea, and they added similar ones to nose rings for draft oxen so any type of toothed bridle or curb came to be called a brake. By 1430 this brake was an essential piece of harness for horse-drawn vehicles.

Mouths of some draft animals became so tough that they paid little attention to the brake. Others sometimes became frightened and ran away with carriages and wagons, no matter how hard drivers pulled on their line. This situation led craftsmen to devise a method by which a block against the rear wheel of a vehicle could be pressed against the wheel by means of a lever. Highly effective, the new gadget gradually became standard equipment.

Helped by the notion of "breaking motion," the name of the old *brake* transferred to modern devices and sticks to them in spite of such innovations as hydraulic action and use of compressed air.

Throw into Stitches

THE language of several early Teutonic peoples included forms of a word meaning "to stick"—as with the point of a knife. Passing through Old English as *stice,* it was later modified to *stitch*. All types of pricks and stabs took that name.

One characteristic stablike pain, caused by acute spasms of rib muscles, is especially prominent after violent exercise. Though no wound is involved, one may hurt almost as though stabbed. Athletes—especially runners—are prone to pains from such a "stitch in the side."

Long ago it was noticed that violent and prolonged laughter may also lead to a stabbing muscular cramp. So the designation for a minor knife wound came to be used for pains from excessive hilarity. It clings in speech with such persistence that an unusually funny story can *throw into stitches* its hearer.

Feel One's Pulse

A SIXTEEN-FOOT roll of Egyptian papyrus dating from about 1550 B.C., but not translated until the 1920s, is one of the oldest documents to describe the process of counting the pulse. Within a few centuries after it was written, Chinese physicians discovered that arteries throb in rhythmic patterns. It's easy for an experienced person to feel pulsations of blood vessels in the wrist, temple, or foot and determine whether the rate is rapid or slow. Chinese of the fifth century B.C. became positively poetic about this phenomenon. A medical text of a somewhat later period declares that "the pulse is like scattered leaves of trees . . . like a taut thread . . . like a bubbling spring."

During centuries when the European physicians of the Middle Ages could do little but investigate the workings of the body on the surface, the pulse was the most important of all diagnostic yard-sticks. Before he attempted any treatment, a good doctor of the fourteenth century would insist that he be permitted to "taste the pulse" of his patient.

So many wrists were felt in attempts to discover clues to health and illness that the physicians' phrase entered general speech. By the 1500s to *feel one's pulse* referred not simply to ascertaining a physical condition but also to discovering the intentions and purposes of another.

Nostril

IN Old English speech *thirl* meant any kind of hole or perfora-tion. Two of the most conspicuous holes seen every day are those in the middle of the human face. Their size and placement are major factors affecting appearance; many women of the fourteenth century esteemed men with even noses and small thirls.

A common process in pronunciation, the transposition of letters, reshaped the word into *thril*. In the *Canterbury Tales* Geoffrey Chaucer described a man whose "nose-thrills were black and wyde." A proverb of about the same period held that "whoso hath the nose-thrills much open, he is strongly angry." In time the word *nostril* evolved.

By the Skin of the Teeth

TRANSLATORS often have difficulty transferring ideas from one language to another, especially if the original text is in an ancient tongue and the two cultures are completely different.

A case in point is in Job 19:20 in the Bible. English scholars who produced the Geneva Bible in 1560 gave a literal rendering of the line describing Job's narrow escape: "I have escaped with the skinne of my tethe." The King James Version of 1611 retained the colorful phrase, and by 1650 anyone who barely missed disaster was likely to say that he escaped *by the skin of the teeth*.

Unimaginative scholars have protested that the teeth have no skin. Their objections are useless; the biblical phrase is too well established to yield in favor of a matter-of-fact substitute. In spite of this some modern translations contain the line, "I have escaped with only my gums," which is not nearly as poetic.

Hunch

UNTIL the rise of scientific medicine, it was generally believed that a deformed person had special links with the demonic world. A gross malformation such as a hump or "hunch" in the spine was considered to be a mark of great psychic powers. Through league with the devil a hunchback was believed capable of seeing into the future. For centuries accurate prediction was strongly linked with possession of a gnarled back. Consequently any premonition or flash of insight came to be known as a *hunch*.

Muscle

EARLY Romans glorified the human body, placing great emphasis upon the beauty of women and the strength of men. In a city's gymnasium youths received rigorous physical training.

Because the rippling of a sinew bears some resemblance to a rodent scurrying under the skin, Romans called it *musculus*, or "little mouse." This word passed into most European languages with minor changes and entered English as "muscule," with passing generations altering the spelling to *muscle*. Especially in the case of the biceps, a system of specialized tissues may bear some resemblance to a little mouse.

Skeleton

AFTER flourishing in great cities of Greece and Rome, the study of medicine reached a peak under Galen of Pergamum, a noted teacher of the second century. His textbooks became so famous that there were no major changes in them for the next 1300 years. The first great modern medical text was published by Andreas Vesalius, father of anatomy, in 1543.

The study of human anatomy quickly surged into prominence on the European continent; however, it did not become a major field of inquiry in England until later. Part of the lag was due to the fact that medical students of the island had no legal source from which to secure bodies for dissection. Many a town physician lived and died without ever seeing the bony framework of the body.

John Banister, a London surgeon prominent during the reign of Elizabeth I, turned to ancient books for information. Late in life he published an ambitious work on "the History of Man, sucked from the sap of the most approved anatomists." In reading Greek manuscripts he had encountered a term for a "mummy." Modified from *skeletos* ("dried up"), it was sometimes spelled *skeleton*.

Banister seized upon this word to use for a system of bones, and it became the standard term for what's left when a body is really dried up.

Feet of Clay

NEBUCHADNEZZAR II was the Babylonian king who captured Jerusalem in 587 B.C., destroyed the city, and took the Hebrew people into captivity, ending the Judean kingdom. The Old Testament tells of his bouts of insanity when he imagined he was an ox and would go into the fields to eat grass.

The book of Daniel tells how the young Hebrew captive explained one of the king's strange dreams. Nebuchadnezzar had seen a giant image with a golden head, silver arms and breast, brass thighs, and iron legs. Every part was metal except the feet, which were compounded partly of iron and partly of potter's clay.

Daniel said that his feet made the metal figure vulnerable, meaning that Babylon would be broken into pieces.

Impressed by this dramatic story, English readers of the Bible seized upon the weak spot of the strange figure as a symbol of weakness in general. Today, any noted person with a vulnerable point is still said to have *feet of clay*.

Tonic

THOUGH numerous types of illness are highly specific, it's not easy to define a state of good health. Physicians of a few centuries ago considered such well-being to rest largely upon proper firmness or tension in organs and tissues. So "tone" was used to designate any general condition. Never very precise, "tone" was a major medical term during much of the seventeenth and eighteenth centuries.

Anything that fostered the rather nebulous "tone of the body" came to be called a "tonic" or "tone enhancer." Fresh air was high on the list of such agencies. Later, iron compounds came into general use as tonic bitters. Though many experts now discount the importance of bodily tension as an index to health, any medicine designed to aid general welfare rather than a precise condition is still known as a *tonic*.

Insulin

CENTURIES-OLD records indicate that people have long suffered from the malady now known as diabetes. Its real nature was not suspected, however, until 1789, when an English physician surmised it might have some connection with a strange tongue-shaped gland found near the middle of the abdomen.

No one had any real understanding of the pancreas or its functions, but eventually it was learned that small islands of special tissue are scattered through it, which scientists called *islets* (or *islands*) *of Laugerhans*. They secrete a chemical that fosters digestion of sugar. Diabetes is caused when the body cannot make normal use of sugar.

In 1922, while working at the University of Toronto, Dr. F. G. Banting was able to isolate from the "islands" of the pancreas the hormone that controls diabetes. He and his colleagues named the substance *insulin* from the Latin word *insula* ("island"). A medical discovery of the first rank, insulin revolutionized the treatment of diabetes and pointed the way to a whole group of related body products now familiar as hormones.

Calf of the Leg

DOMESTIC cows have been vital to western civilization, though milk did not become an important commercial commodity until recent generations. Steers were work animals for centuries, while meat and leather were essentials for living.

Long ago, householders and farmers became fascinated with unusual qualities of young bovines. As early as the eighth century, such an animal was known as a *cealf* and was welcomed as an addition to a man's assets. Especially when born to a cow who has been poorly fed, a calf displays muscles that ripple under the skin and cluster in prominent knots.

Those who worked in the fields noticed that behind the shank of the human leg several big muscles cluster close together, a formation having so much in common with those in young animals that it came to be called the *calf of the leg*.

Geoffrey Chaucer was not paying a compliment when he painted a word portrait that included the comment, "Full longe were his legges and full lene like a staff . . . there was no calf."

Guts

UNTIL recent times it was believed that the viscera were the seat of human emotions and attitudes. As late as the 1600s a person experiencing deep grief described himself as "grieved to the guts."

Earlier generations had referred to the internal organs as "pluck," probably because when animals are dressed, their innards are "plucked" out of the carcass. Since the pluck was regarded as the seat of courage and determination, a brave man was termed "plucky."

Originally a polite word, "pluck" gradually came to be regarded as vulgar, and "guts" was substituted. It became common to say that a courageous person had guts rather than pluck.

"Guts" soon suffered the same fate as "pluck" and is now avoided in polite speech. However, *guts* has been retained as a slang term for unusual courage or a visceral response.

Have One's Heart in the Right Place

EGYPTIAN priests who prepared mummies for burial were among the first persons to have an accurate knowledge of the heart's size and location. However, much knowledge was lost with the decay of ancient civilizations, and an accurate knowledge of anatomy did not reach England until the seventeenth century. Neither ancient lore nor more recent discoveries have had the slightest effect upon speech customs that treated the heart as a wandering rather than a fixed organ. A fearful person was long described as "having his heart at the bottom of his hose" or as "having his heart in his mouth." An easily offended person is still said to "wear his heart on his sleeve."

During the 1600s another descriptive phrase surged into wide use, and in the space age it shows no indication of dropping out of speech. In spite of the findings of physiologists, we still say that anyone with good intentions is properly made and, therefore, "has his heart in the right place."

CHAPTER 14

EDUCATION

ALPHABET

DEAN

CURRICULUM

GLOSSARY

CANCEL / CANCELLATION

POSTHASTE

SHEEPSKIN

FACULTY

COMMENCEMENT

POSER

CRISSCROSS

ACADEMY

BARBARIAN

ORIENTATION

BY THE GRAPEVINE

Alphabet

REVIVAL of interest in classical language and thought caused teachers to give special emphasis to Greek. In that tongue *alpha* names the first character in the set of letters and *beta* stands for the second. Ancient Greeks used these two symbols to stand for the whole set of letters they used in writing, much as we say a child "learns his ABCs."

Frequent use of the two first letters of the Greek system led to their being joined in popular speech so that *alphabet* names any complete pattern of written symbols, ancient or modern.

Dean

THE basic organization of the imperial army of the late Roman Empire was a unit of ten men. The man in charge of nine subordinates was a *decanus*, from *decem* ("ten"). The Roman Catholic Church used the same division in monasteries during the Middle Ages. The head of a group of ten monks was a *decant*. In English the word became *dean*.

Gradually the meaning expanded. In the church it refers to the head of the chapter of canons governing a cathedral or a priest appointed to oversee a group of parishes. In education it refers to an administrative officer in charge of a division of a university or the officer of a college or high school who counsels students and enforces rules. It can also mean a senior member of a group, such as "the dean of the Washington press corps."

Curriculum

WHEN not engaged in war, Roman troops amused themselves with games and sports. Among the favorite contests was racing a chariot, or *currus*. Early speedsters eventually modified this two-wheel racer and devised a light vehicle they called *curriculum* ("little chariot"). It was used so extensively that its name attached to the track, or course, on which it was driven.

With the fall of Rome, the sporting term disappeared and remained dormant until the Renaissance and the revival of interest in classical times. Learned men in Scottish universities borrowed the old racetrack word and used it to stand for the round of training along which they drove their students. Popularized by this usage, *curriculum* entered common speech in the seventeenth century as the designation for the courses of study in an educational institution.

Glossary

MEDIEVAL monks patiently copied the Bible by hand and frequently encountered a word that they considered so difficult that an explanation was needed. Since Latin was then the universal language of scholarship, such a word was called *glossa* ("a word requiring explanation"). The explanation itself came to be known as a "gloss," which was customarily written in the margin, near the word it explained.

Eventually a large number of glosses were collected into a separate volume, or *glossary*. Printers of books later borrowed the monks' term to stand for any list of technical words and their meanings.

Cancel / Cancellation

MONKS produced practically all written material of the Middle Ages. They worked under many difficulties; parchment was expensive and hard to get, and there were no erasers. When a man made an error in copying, he dared not try to scrape off the ink with a knife because it might ruin his parchment.

It became customary to draw crossed lines through matter in which an error occurred. Such lines bore a strong resemblance to a lattice; hence, the monks called them *cancelli* (Latin for "lattices"). Introduction of modern writing materials has made many changes in civilization, but our terms *cancel* and *cancellation* commemorate the little lattices of medieval scribes.

Posthaste

RAPID transmission of important messages has been a matter of concern since early times. Royal couriers were organized by such diverse peoples as the Chinese, Incas, and Persians. Before the beginning of the present era, the Romans had elaborate systems to handle imperial letters.

Ordinary folk could not avail themselves of such facilities though.

Under leadership of the University of Paris, the world's first public mail service was launched in the thirteenth century. Men and horses were kept at special places; from Latin for "station" such a point was called a "post." The English borrowed the post system and used it first for transmission of the king's packet. The spread of education produced many more persons who could read and write letters, so by 1635 the post was so widely used on the island that regular rates for public correspondence were established.

Those who wrote letters considered them important, and they were always eager to speed them on their way. Hence, it became customary to write across the face of a letter, "Haste, post, haste!" Thus *posthaste* came to mean "in a hurry"—whether connected with letters or not.

Sheepskin

FOR writing material the ancient Egyptians used papyrus made from reeds that grew in marshes of the Nile River. This was the preferred writing material until around A.D. 300 when parchment made from the skins of sheep, goats, and other animals, took over. The art of papermaking reached Europe from the East by 1100, and by 1500 paper had almost replaced parchment. This coincided with the invention of the printing press. Nevertheless colleges and universities continued to cling to the custom of preparing "graduation parchments." The actual skin of the animal was used as late as the middle of the nineteenth century, and most diplomas were written in Latin. Whether or not he could read the roll of parchment that certified he had won his degree, a college graduate of the era regarded this as one of his most important possessions.

Born as a slang expression for "diploma" among American students, the name *sheepskin* remains alive in spite of the fact that most sheepskins are now machine-printed on heavy paper rather than hand-lettered on parchment.

Faculty

FROM Latin for "power or ability," an ancient term passed through French and entered English as "faculty" and was in general use by 1490. The sense of "capacity to do something" is still preserved in the word when we say a fully competent person "has all his faculties."

With the rise of colleges and universities, deans and chancellors sought adept and facile persons as teachers. As a result a group of men fully competent to teach was known collectively as a "faculty." The title indicated "the whole body of masters and doctors" with special ability in the four traditional departments of study: theology, law, medicine, and arts.

While some students may question the ability of their professors, the venerable term of respect is still very much alive. In

modern usage any body of men and women engaged in teaching
any subjects to students of whatever age constitutes a *faculty*.

Commencement

IT seems strange that *commencement* refers to the ceremony at
which academic degrees or diplomas are conferred. "Finishment"
would seem to be more logical. Yet the word was appropriate earlier,
as medieval universities required their graduates to spend a period
teaching beginners. Commencement, therefore, did not mean that a
man was released from an institution but that he ceased to be a pupil
and commenced to teach.

Poser

BY the sixteenth century English schools commonly gave
strict examinations. A special officer known as the "apposer,"
meaning "examiner," framed the questions to test the students.
Many a fellow must have performed this task effectively, for the
examiner's title was clipped to *poser* and became the term for a
baffling question or problem.

Crisscross

IN the sixteenth and seventeenth centuries, the hornbook was
the major educational tool for very young children. Actually not a
book, it was a sheet of paper fastened to a board with a handle and
covered with thin, translucent horn to protect it.

Printed on the paper were the alphabet in large and small letters,
the Benediction, the Lord's Prayer, and the Roman numerals. A
cross was placed at the beginning of the sheet as a tribute to the
Savior.

Little scholars tried to copy this "Christ cross" or "Christ's cross"
as well as the letters that followed it. Just as the pronunciation of

"Christ's mass" became "Christmas," so this became "crisscross." By the late 1700s any pattern of crossed lines had come to be called a *crisscross*.

Academy

IN 387 B.C. Plato founded a school of philosophy and science in Athens that became known as "the Academy." It was in a grove that according to legend had been given to a man named Academus at the time of the Trojan War. The Academy is often called the first university. Subjects such as astronomy, mathematics, political science, and the biological sciences were discussed there. Plato's great pupil Aristotle was a student. Its influence is felt today, for we still use *academy* to name institutions as diversified as the Academy of Motion Picture Arts and Sciences and the U.S. Academy at West Point.

Barbarian

HISTORIANS pay tribute to ancient Greece as the world's greatest center of culture and learning. Their judgment is not new; the Greeks themselves were proudly confident that they excelled in every area of life. Arrogance ran so high that they sneeringly referred to the speech of non-Greeks as made up of unintelligible sounds, like "bar-bar." Consequently, any foreigner came to be called *barbarus*.

Passing through Latin the label of contempt eventually entered English as *barbarian*. Little changed by centuries of usage; the term of mockery is now applied to any rude or savage person. Its long record indicates that in every age and among all peoples many take it for granted that anyone who speaks with an unfamiliar accent can't possibly have anything significant to say.

Orientation

ORIENTATION week has become a familiar institution on the college campus. Many industries have adopted a similar period of "breaking in" new employees. Though such formal practice of orientation is modern in origin, it represents the latest in a long chain of developments.

During the Crusades in which Christian Europe tried to recapture the Holy Land from its Moslem conquerors, religious zeal made east the key direction. From an ancient term for "direction of the sun's rising" the East was known as "the Orient." Medieval cathedrals were built with their long axis due east-west with the chief chancel or altar at the orient or eastern end. Pious folk frequently insisted on being buried with their feet pointing east. As late as 1775 mapmakers marked the east with a cross.

From the process of pointing to the Orient, or getting one's bearings, *orientation* came to signify all types of alignment whether toward the geographical Orient or some other direction in ideas or space.

By the Grapevine

SAMUEL F. B. Morse made history when he sent the first telegraph message on May 24, 1844. Americans, amazed at "what God hath wrought," clamored for the quick new means of communication. Within seven years half a hundred companies had lines in operation. Henry David Thoreau, pausing in his wanderings about Walden Pond, wondered whether men had anything to say that was worth transmitting by electricity.

He was virtually alone in his skepticism. All over the country workmen hastily strung wires between sagging poles and opened telegraph offices. One line, constructed in 1859, set something of a record. It extended from Placerville, California, to Virginia City and was so crudely strung that practical jokers compared it with a grapevine.

Perhaps the new expression would have died a natural death had it not become linked with field dispatches in the Civil War. In addition to authentic telegraph messages, there were many wild rumors, which spread so rapidly it seemed there must be a "grapevine telegraph" at work. It was fixed in Yankee lingo by both true and false bits of news from battlefields, so it became customary to say that any person-to-person report is transmitted *by the grapevine.*

CHAPTER 15

PIONEERS AND COWPOKES

PAN

ROUGHNECK

WASHOUT

ALSO RAN

CASKET

A HARD ROW TO HOE

STUMP

HAVE AN EAR TO THE
GROUND

HAIR-RAISING

TOUCH WITH A
TEN-FOOT POLE

JAMBOREE

BONANZA

AT THE DROP OF A HAT

FIGHT FIRE WITH FIRE

CINCH

CUT NO ICE

PUT THE BEE ON

SIT ON THE
ANXIOUS SEAT

CHINAMAN'S CHANCE

DON'T TAKE ANY
WOODEN NICKELS

CROOK

MAKE THE FUR FLY

CON MAN

Pan

MINERS in other parts of the world developed methods of washing gold-bearing soil by hand. It remained for U.S. prospectors, however, to reduce the use of mining pans to a science. Skillful movements with the wrist could result in surprising efficiency— washing out practically all dirt and impurities.

This process of sifting was soon compared with critical evaluation of human performances. Just as the miner frequently washed soil without finding gold, the critic was sometimes hard put to discover merit in drama or literature. When nothing good could be said about a production, it was described as "panned out"; hence, the analyst was said to *pan* the effort.

Roughneck

LANDED gentry of colonial times attempted to transplant European culture to the New World. Many of them ordered their knee breeches from London tailors, and their homes were stocked with imported finery. Their hair styles reflected the latest Continental fashions. In order to be well groomed, a gentleman had to keep his long locks in a queue, neatly trimmed, powdered, and tied.

A frontiersman seldom had time for such foolishness. Many a fellow gathered his hair in a crude knot that was laced with a strip of rawhide. When it grew long enough to be annoying, he was likely to whack it off with a hunting knife in such fashion that rough-cut hair hung down his neck. Such a *roughneck* might be rude and boisterous, so his name came to label any bully or rowdy, regardless of the style of his hairdo.

Washout

EARLY U.S. gold mining made large use of water to separate precious metal from dirt. Sluice boxes were built along many streams, permitting bulk handling of ore. Where water was scarce, pans were in vogue. In either case it was the miner's object to remove all earth and leave gold behind.

When a claim began to play out or new diggings were opened, a day's work sometimes left the sluice box bare. In such a case the ore was a literal *washout*. Miners evidently saw many a box washed clean, for the vivid expression was soon applied to any sort of failure or calamity.

Also Ran

IN most horse races judges do not determine the order in which all the animals finish. They simply clock the first three across the line.

Newspapers of the nineteenth century naturally gave prominence to horses that placed in important races. They frequently described all three animals, gave their time, listed their owners, and listed their winnings. Toward the end of such a story it was customary to mention horses that also ran.

During the third quarter of the century U.S. presidential elections came to resemble horse races. Many new parties were organized: Greenback, Anti-Monopoly, United Labor, National Silver, Prohibition, American, and others. Their candidates seldom gave any serious competition to men selected by old-line parties. After elections newspapers dismissed many an obscure aspirant for the presidency as an *also ran*—one who didn't come close enough to winning to have his order determined. By 1900 the expression had come to be applied to any person badly beaten in competition of any sort.

Casket

DIVERSITY in size and shape of containers is a modern development. As late as medieval times, the chief container used in commerce was the wooden cask. A few years before Columbus sailed for the West Indies, someone invented a small metal cask for holding jewels, money, and valuable documents. A forerunner of the safe-deposit box, the cask came to be called a little cask, or "casket," because of its shape and size.

English usage still makes "casket" stand for a money box. In America the word went through a period of transition about the time of the Civil War. Persons who wished to avoid the use of so blunt a term as "coffin" began to use "casket" as a substitute. Nathaniel Hawthorne attacked the usage, complaining that it compels a person to shrink from being buried at all.

In spite of Hawthorne's objection, Americans forgot the real meaning of *casket* and began using it exclusively as a term for a death box.

A Hard Row to Hoe

EUROPEANS who came to America as colonists found the new country to have a great deal of level, fertile farm land, but some settlers pushed away from the coast into the foothills of the Appalachian Mountains. Many a pioneer built his cabin in a remote spot where plowing was difficult because of the terrain. Matters were further complicated by the scarcity of work animals and gear. Hence, the backwoods farmer in such regions as the Kentucky border leaned heavily on hand labor. These farmers usually had large families, and every member was expected to wield a hoe many days each year.

Monotonous at best, such labor was likely to become very distasteful toward the close of a warm day. A youngster working against his will was likely to beg relief and complain that he had a *hard row to hoe*. Hence, the phrase came to stand for any difficult or unpleasant task.

Stump

THOUGH U.S. pioneers built their houses and barns of logs, trees were so thick that they were regarded as a nuisance. It was hard enough to cut and burn the trees themselves, and their stumps created even more serious problems.

Frontiersmen frequently helped one another in clearing new ground. After a log rolling it was necessary to come back and pull up as many stumps as possible. Some men prided themselves on their skill in getting out the big ones, but it was not unusual for a boaster to suffer defeat at the hands of a stubborn stump. As a result anything that proved beyond a person's capacities was said to *stump* him.

Have An Ear to the Ground

NO region in the world has stimulated more red-blooded fiction than the American West. Indians figure in these stories to such an extent that the redskin has emerged into modern literature as a stock character. He is a superb hunter and a fearless warrior. Untouched by civilization, he has developed his senses to an amazing degree. For example, he hears so well that when he suspects the approach of an enemy, he puts his ear to the ground and listens for the sound of men or horses. Especially in stony regions, he can readily determine just how many are coming and how far away they are.

There is no evidence that Indians ever listened for a footfall a mile or so away. Fiction writers made so many allusions to the practice that by 1900 it was familiar to every reader of pioneer yarns. Consequently, a person who listens for faint noises or watches for signs of a change in public sentiment is said to *have an ear to the ground.*

Hair-Raising

As a synonym for "frightful," *hair-raising* is one of the most striking labels in modern speech. The term has been in use only a few generations. Pioneers and soldiers who fought the American Indians were horrified when they first learned that Indians scalped their victims, but early in American history whites also adopted the practice. Scalps of slain Indians were turned in when their killers wished to collect the bounty offered by authorities. Shaping a grim joke, Indian fighters began to speak of scalping as "lifting the hair," or "hair-raising."

This bloody practice was largely abandoned when peace treaties were signed with the Indians. Nevertheless, "hair-raising" had made so strong an impact upon speech that the term remained in the language to indicate an extremely frightful experience. Helped by association with reactions of startled dogs and cats, it's now applied to humans in spite of the fact that it has been thousands of years since ordinary persons have had muscles that could pull their hair erect when frightened.

Touch with a Ten-Foot Pole

When a person is unwilling to become involved in a project, he is likely to say he won't touch it with a ten-foot pole. It seems odd that we should always specify that length rather than sometimes referring to a nine- or a twelve-foot piece.

Reasons for stipulating a ten-foot pole are buried deep in American history. Pioneers who pushed into frontier country learned to make good use of rivers, swamps, and lakes. Special pole boats with flat bottoms were used for hauling everything from household goods to bales of cotton. Deep water was dangerous; currents could snatch a clumsy pole boat and dash it against rocks or throw it upon a mud bar. So it became standard practice for boatmen to cut their poles just ten feet long, then use them to measure depth as well as to push.

In river towns and farm communities alike, a person wishing to avoid a situation would say he wouldn't *touch it with a ten-foot pole* of a river man. The expression became so firmly fixed that it survives long after modern vessels put pole boats out of business.

Jamboree

DURING the roaring decades when the American frontier was really wild and woolly, many odd words were coined. If they ever had much rhyme or reason, students of speech have been unable to uncover the circumstances of their formation. One such queer character is the word "jamboree," which sounds as though it may have been modeled after "whoopee."

First used on the frontier around 1850, the colorful word came to stand for any spectacular party, elaborate outing, or prolonged spree. Such an artificial term should have died in a few generations. It dropped into obscurity and might have died had not Lord Baden-Powell, founder of the Boy Scouts, planned an international rally in 1920.

He and his associates felt the great gathering needed a distinctive name; someone suggested that it be given the frontier name of *jamboree.* Extensive publicity about this and later Scout rallies gave new vigor to the vagabond of speech, and the made-up term for a wild backwoods spree became the standard title for any elaborate convention.

Bonanza

As long as ships were at the mercy of winds, fair weather was highly prized. From the Latin word *bonus,* meaning good, evolved the word *bonanza*, used by Spanish sailors to name clear days after a hard blow.

In time the sea term came to indicate good fortune in general. During the California gold rush beginning in 1848, American miners borrowed the term from the Spanish with whom they came in contact. It became a household word after one of the world's greatest gold rushes took place in the Yukon Territory of northwest Canada, beginning in 1896. Today *bonanza* applies to any source of great wealth or prosperity.

At the Drop of a Hat

DUELING by prescribed rules was common in the United States until the mid-1800s, although the various states began to outlaw it, beginning with Tennessee in 1801. In one of the most famous duels, Aaron Burr, the vice president of the United States, killed Alexander Hamilton, former secretary of the treasury.

According to the dueling code, the man challenged had the choice of weapons, and usually they were pistols in America. Each duelist chose a friend to act as a "second," and a surgeon often attended. To avoid the law officers, the meetings often took place at dawn in a forest clearing. The duelists stood back to back and marched an agreed number of paces in opposite directions. Then one of the seconds dropped a handkerchief, and the fighters turned and fired.

On the frontier disagreements were settled much more informally. Participants used guns, knives, whips, or fists—and they often fought in broad daylight before an audience. The referee would drop a hat (often more readily available than a handkerchief) to start the fight.

The phrase *at the drop of a hat,* meaning impatient to begin a fight or other undertaking, apparently was first used in the West around 1887.

Fight Fire with Fire

FIRE was a fearful foe of householders on the American frontier. Most cabins were built in small clearings, but grass and brush might extend nearly to the doors. Disaster threatened whenever flames pushed by the wind approached. In this situation settlers often set backfires. This meant burning a strip in the path of a big blaze then extinguishing the fire to leave barren ground that would not burn. To *fight fire with fire* was a desperate venture, for the control strip might get out of hand and add to the danger instead of reducing it. Consequently, the frontier term has come to indicate any emergency measure that involves great hazard.

Cinch

CITY-BRED adventurers who flocked to the California gold fields in 1849 encountered many odd customs, one of which was a novel saddle girth. Instead of using English-style bellybands with straps and buckles, Indians and Mexicans of the Southwest employed twisted horsehair ropes running between two rings.

Such a piece of gear, which the Spanish called *cincha*, was more adjustable than any equipment familiar in the East. A rider who knew how to fasten a cinch could lace a saddle so it would stay in position all day. Clumsy buckles had to be adjusted at frequent intervals. The holding power of the *cinch* was so great that its name entered common speech to stand for any sure thing.

Cut No Ice

BEFORE modern refrigeration, ice was not available in warm climates and during the summer in cooler places.

Around 1806 Frederic Tudor decided to ship ice to warmer regions where it did not form in the winter. Friends scoffed, but he went ahead with his idea of treating ice as a crop. He packed the blocks of ice in sawdust and carried them on speedy merchant ships. Within a few years he made a fortune from his sales to New Orleans, Havana, Charleston, Savannah, and other cities.

Soon many competitors entered the field. Using special long-bladed saws, they put their crews to work in the dead of winter. Employees spent as much time as possible warming their hands at campfires. Caught at such a practice, an ice-cutter would declare that he was merely getting ready to go back to work.

His employer was likely to berate him, declaring that such use of his time *cut no ice*. From this literal use of the phrase it became standard to apply it to any act that accomplishes nothing and influences no one.

Put the Bee On

SETTLERS along the Atlantic Coast of North America were delighted to find wild bees plentiful. When the household cook needed a sweetening agent, the father or one of the older boys could almost always find a bee tree. The settlers noticed that the tiny insects always worked in groups, and they began to call any communal gathering that combined work and pleasure a "bee." Ladies had their spinning bees and quilting bees, men their husking bees, and entire communities had spelling bees.

Money was scarce on the frontier, so when churches were organized, congregations were seldom able to give the preacher a cash salary. Instead, they organized "bees" for him. All members of the community, whether they attended church or not, were solicited for gifts of work, clothing, or food.

Sponsors of a bee were not slow to put pressure on reluctant contributors. The result was that any person who made a determined request for a gift was said to *put the bee on* his victim. Later the term expanded to include persistent demands for loans and personal favors as well as gifts.

Sit on the Anxious Seat

FRONTIER evangelists and circuit riders were as rough and ready as the trappers, hunters, and settlers to whom they preached. Such religionists found that dramatic conversions took place in an atmosphere of emotional tension. Hence, it became customary for the backwoods preacher to provide a special place for listeners "coming under conviction" and visibly anxious about their spiritual welfare. In many a brush arbor and camp meeting, such persons gathered on a special "anxious bench" or "anxious seat" while pondering their need for salvation.

Around the time of Andrew Jackson's presidency, astute observers made political applications of the religious term. As a result, by the 1840s any man who occupied a seat in Congress but was uncertain of reelection was said to *sit on the anxious seat*. Spreading from political circles, the vivid American-born phrase came into general use to name any uncertain or precarious position.

Chinaman's Chance

OUR familiar expression, *Chinaman's chance*, acquired its present meaning of no chance at all in the lawless days of the old West. White ruffians were ruthlessly brutal in their dealings with the Orientals who had immigrated to build the railroads. If an Asian was caught in a petty crime, he was likely to be strung to the nearest tree. Neither public opinion nor frontier courts gave the Chinaman an opportunity for legal redress—he literally had no chance for justice.

Don't Take Any Wooden Nickels

EARLY Yankee tradesmen showed the same skill and tenacity that has led their descendants to be credited with the ability to sell refrigerators to the Eskimos. Some of them cracked jokes about peddling wooden substitutes for good merchandise, while others did it when they could. In 1832 the *Boston Transcript* warned: "We recently read of wooden hams in some parts of the west neatly sewed up in canvass, said to have their origin with the same ingenious people who invented wooden nutmegs."

It was believed that some fellows, unwilling to do an honest day's work, would go to the trouble of making wooden nickels. That was considerable trouble to go to for such a small amount of money. Whether or not any phony nickels were ever made, it became proverbial that greenhorns had better watch out for them. The jocular warning *don't take any wooden nickels* remains in speech as a memorial to the ingenuity of swindlers, the imagination of tale spinners, or both.

Crook

SEVERAL types of rail fences were common in frontier America. The zigzag variety—sometimes called the "worm" or "snake" fence—was the easiest to build. Farms and pastures were frequently guarded by these crude barriers. It became commonplace to compare a person who refused to follow the straight and narrow path with a fence and brand him as "crooked." In 1879 a *Chicago Tribune* story used *crook* to name a swindler or thief.

Make the Fur Fly

SOME adventurers who flocked to the New World in search of riches realized enormous profits from trapping. They discovered many creatures not known in their native countries. Some yielded luxurious pelts, but one abundant little animal had fur so coarse it was hardly worth taking.

Raccoon pelts were used chiefly for making rough caps. Coons were so plentiful that backwoods bullies hunted them for the sport of seeing them die under the teeth of their dogs. When two or three hounds attacked simultaneously, they would literally fill the air with bits of fur from their prey. Such fights were usually short but furious. Consequently, a frontiersman was said to *make the fur fly* when he sailed into an opponent like a dog attacking a coon.

Con Man

HARD times following the Civil War forced criminals to resort to all sorts of tricks to gain relatively small amounts of money. One of the most common was the sale of fraudulent mining stock. Investors were reluctant to advance funds without examining property, so swindlers adopted the practice of asking a victim to make a small deposit "just as a gesture of confidence." The full amount was to be paid only after a trip to the West on the part of the purchaser.

A swindler would take the money advanced and decamp. This type of trick became known as the "confidence game" because it worked only if the victim had confidence in the proposal. Anyone who practiced confidence games came to be called a *con man*. This title was applied to many types of swindlers and is still used to designate a shrewd thief who finds suckers by means of the Internet or e-mail.

CHAPTER 16

MALES AND FEMALES

FLIRT

WEDLOCK

CURTAIN LECTURE

SET ONE'S CAP AT

MONKEY

HUSBAND

WIFE

BRIDEGROOM

FATHOM

TIE THE KNOT

PARAPHERNALIA

GOSSIP

NICKNAME

Flirt

UNTIL the middle of the eighteenth century the term "flirt" was used as a verb, in the sense of "to move jerkily." One day at a gathering of the cream of London society, several men hovered around a vivacious young widow, who shot first one, then another, an engaging smile. As they talked, she flirted her fan back and forth.

Lord Chesterfield, who was present, observed Lady Frances Shirley, assessed the situation, and snorted, "It's plain she's flirting." The term quickly entered standard speech, so now anyone who makes playfully romantic overtures or deals with a situation in a trifling or superficial manner is call a *flirt*.

Wedlock

MEDIEVAL parish registers listed unmarried men as *solutus* (Latin for "loose, unchained").

Contrary to logic, the term *wedlock* didn't originally refer to a union locked by the wedding ceremony. Rather, it's a survival of Anglo-Saxon *wedd* ("pledge") and *lac* (noun denoting activity). Early *wedlac* was the money or other property given to the groom by the bride's father. In return for the money the bridegroom promised to take the lass in marriage. Transferring to the marriage vow, or obligation, *wedlock* came to mean the state of marital union.

Curtain Lecture

MANY women know that a man would rather be scolded at any other time than when he is trying to go to sleep. No matter what he has done, he never feels that a bedtime scolding, or *curtain lecture*, is in order.

The phrase indicates that the practice is of ancient lineage, for until modern times it was customary to hang curtains on four-poster beds. Two or more couples frequently slept in one room, and the wife who had a grievance usually waited until the curtains were drawn about the bed to begin scolding her spouse.

Furniture styles have changed, but human nature has not. So the *curtain lecture*—without curtain—remains a familiar institution.

Set One's Cap At

A GIRL eager to win a particular man is likely to be accused of setting her cap at him. This phrase goes back to the time when France was a major power with a powerful navy and large fleets of commercial vessels.

French sailors called the head of their ship its *cap*, from the Latin *caput* ("head"). When a steersman was ordered to head for a particular point, he *set the cap* of the ship toward the goal. Eventually, the old term for sailing toward a definite spot became attached to activities of a woman who sought to win the man of her choice.

Monkey

FOLK sayings of many nations include references to the talkativeness of women. Most of these sayings were probably originated by husbands who wished to take a sly dig at their mates.

This attitude was reflected by Italians who cast about for a suitable name for a strange little animal that had been introduced from Africa. Shriveled and grotesquely ugly, the little creature walked about on its hind legs and chattered incessantly. Men who saw it agreed that it resembled nothing so much as a prattling old woman. Hence, they gave the beast their nickname for such a dame, *monicchia*. Passing through French into English, the spelling changed to *monkey*.

Husband

HOME ownership by average persons is a modern development. Until the close of feudal times, the masses were peasants
who lived in rough cottages that belonged to their masters. In rank
above them were yeomen who were an independent class of small
landowners and farmers. Such a man was termed a *husband*, from
hus ("house") and *bunda* ("owner of land and stock").

Since a husband occupied a social and economic position
well above that of a serf, he was an attractive matrimonial
catch. Ambitious mothers were eager for their girls to win husbands. By the thirteenth century the title had come to stand for
any man joined to a woman in marriage, whether a homeowner
or not.

Wife

THOUGH by no means her only task, weaving (known as
wifan) was a major occupation of an Anglo-Saxon woman. There
was a general term for humankind, *mann*. In order to distinguish
between the sexes, the female was known as a *wifemann*, or
"weaving human."

In time it became customary for a man to speak of the woman
with whom he lived and who did his weaving, as his wifemann.
Over the centuries the word was shortened to *wife*.

Bridegroom

MODERN usage makes the word "groom" stand for a male
servant or stableboy responsible for the care of horses. In ancient
times anyone who performed menial tasks was given that name.

Many marriage ceremonies were followed by a feast that sometimes lasted several days. In parts of rural Europe the newly married man was expected to act as waiter to his bride during the feast.
Because he played the role of servant to the bride, he was called

the "bride's groom." Contracted in popular speech, the expression became *bridegroom,* and now it is often shortened further back to groom.

Fathom

A FATHOM, the standard nautical measurement of depth, is six feet. The word comes from the Saxon *faethm* ("outstretched arms"). An act of Parliament once defined the term as "the length of a man's arms around the object of his affections."

Tie the Knot

IN some parts of the world, until recent times, the taking of a wife did not necessarily involve going before a clergyman, priest, or civic official. Especially in the East, the family patriarch performed most religious and civil functions.

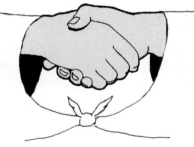

In many places the patriarch performed the marriage ceremony quite simply. He would lay his hands on the bride and groom in blessing, then knot together their sleeves or two corners of their flowing robes. No vows were exchanged; to *tie the knot* symbolized the permanence of the union.

Paraphernalia

UNTIL modern times—and still in some parts of the world—
a bride's family had to provide her husband with a dowry. Such a
marriage settlement became the personal property of the man. He
could dispose of it as he pleased, and even at his death his wife
could not claim it. The wife owned absolutely nothing.

Under Roman law, however, a woman's personal property other
than the dowry remained under her control. Her husband could
exercise no rights over it, and when he died, it was not included in
his estate.

Such property was called *parapherna*, from the Latin word for
"beside dowry." Women's rights in parapherna were included in
most western European codes, which were based on Roman law.

Though there were exceptions, such belongings usually consisted of jewelry, furniture, clothing, and odds and ends. As a result,
the word came to stand for any miscellaneous collection of fur-
nishings. Legislation concerning property rights of women made
the term obsolete in its legal sense, so *paraphernalia* now stands for
any group of articles a man or woman might accumulate.

Gossip

WOMEN are accused of being more prone to gossip than men,
but the history of the word indicates that the sexes are equally
guilty. Though the practice of talking about one another is
probably as old as speech, Anglo-Saxon customs produced the
modern expression. Saxons spoke of any relative as a *sibb*; hence,
a sponsor in baptism was known as a *godsibb* of the infant. Slurred
in popular speech, the term became "gossip."

Ceremonies made it necessary for godparents, or gossips, to
meet several times before and after a baptismal service. It was natural that such gatherings should be clearinghouses for community
news. As a result *gossip* came to be attached to all newsmongers
and idle talkers.

Nickname

LIKE modern parents, some parents of bygone eras gave their babies long names. They abbreviated the names for ordinary use, so that young Williams were called Will. Since they were bestowed in childhood, such shortened names were usually called a "nurse name."

Sometimes an adult retained his nurse name or was given a special name because of some prominent trait or quality. Such a name attached to him over and above his baptismal name. So it was called an *ekename*, from the Saxon for "also."

Slurred over in common speech, an *ekename* became a *nekename* and finally a *nickname*, the "also name" which the gang bestows upon Alfred or Franklin to make him "Red" or "Buddy."

CHAPTER 17

AMBITIOUS AND ENTREPRENEURIAL

BAUD

PANTS

BOBBIES

CZAR / KAISER / JULY

TEDDY BEAR

PULLMAN

CINCHONA

TAWDRY

MAUDLIN

PRALINE

SEQUOIA

DOILY

VARNISH

JIMMY

GUY

TIGHT AS DICK'S
   HATBAND

GOBLIN

MELBA TOAST/
   PEACH MELBA

MAE WEST

SILHOUETTE

MARTINET

Baud

AT his death in 1903, French engineer Jean Maurice Emile Baudot was unknown outside a small circle of engineers and physicists. Yet with the last two letters dropped, his surname is today widely used throughout the world.

Baudot was a pioneer in the then-novel field of binary information. He developed a slow but workable system of transmitting such information, and as a result his abbreviated name came to designate a unit of speed. Capability of transmitting one unit element—usually a bit—per second came to be measured in bauds.

The speed of this process was initially expressed in digits ranging from 1 to 12, so when modems reached the speed of 1,200 bauds per second, many users regarded this as ultimate. A majority of today's modems transmit at least 56,600 bits per second and for convenience are designated as having a speed of 56.6. If Jean Baudot were alive and well, he would find it hard to believe that his abbreviated name has become universally familiar to persons who have never heard of him.

Pants

A CHRISTIAN Roman doctor named Pantaleon was martyred because of his faith in A.D. 305 and later became a saint, the patron of physicians and protector of Venice. Somehow his name—now spelled with a final *e* in sixteenth-century Italian—became attached to a character in the *commedia dell' arte*, a form of slapstick using stock characters.

This comic Pantaleone wore spectacles, slippers, and a lower garment that consisted of both breeches and stockings—all in one piece. Such attire was so distinctive that it eventually took the name of the saint. Modified in English to "pantaloons," it was applied to loose-fitting breeches, then was abbreviated to *pants* as a designation for trousers in general.

Bobbies

ENGLISH aristocrat Sir Robert Peel served in many capacities of public service before he became prime minister in 1834 and again in 1841. His name lives on in an unusual way. Until 1829 London had no regular police force, just ineffectual local constables.

As home secretary, Peel persuaded Parliament to pass the Metropolitan Police Act; then he established a professional police force. Since Sir Robert's admirers called him Bobby, the police came to be known as "Bobby's men" in honor of their founder. The name was soon shortened to *bobbies*, as it still survives today.

Czar/Kaiser/July

JULIUS Caesar may be the only ruler who is commemorated by more than one common word. Although a monarch without a crown, Caesar established a new imperial form of government. After his death his successors took his surname as a title, retaining it until the fall of the Roman Empire. European countries later adopted the name, with minor changes in spelling. Both the Russian *czar* and the German *kaiser* evolved from the word *caesar*.

In 46 B.C. Julius Caesar spearheaded the reform of the calendar, which had become about three months out of synch with the season. The new Julian calendar remained in effect for 1,500 years. After Caesar's death the Romans renamed the month Quintilis in his honor, giving us July.

Teddy Bear

IT'S common knowledge that the Teddy bear got its name from President Theodore Roosevelt, but the chain of circumstances that produced the popular toy is not widely known.

Toy bears were first widely advertised in America in 1902, the year Roosevelt went on a big hunt in Mississippi. While in the woods his dogs found a bear so young that the great hunter refused to shoot it.

Not yet conservation wise, many sportsmen made fun of such sentimental tenderheartedness. For a time Roosevelt was the butt of many jokes. A famous cartoonist sketched Teddy, gun in hand, with his back turned on a small bruin.

People began to associate toys with the incident, so in a matter of months the *Teddy bear* was being featured throughout the nation.

Pullman

OVERNIGHT sleeping cars drawn by locomotives derived their name from that of their inventor George Mortimer Pullman.

It took a long chain of events to put his surname into the stream of speech. Pullman experimented in building cars for sleeping just before the Civil War, but he couldn't sell his idea. Though he had no success, he couldn't turn the idea loose. Back in Chicago after a stint as a storekeeper in a Colorado mining town, he invested twenty thousand dollars—everything he had—and eventually completed the costly and luxurious *Pioneer*.

Everyone acquainted with the *Pioneer* agreed that it was not only ornate and elaborate, it was actually comfortable. Still, the novel railroad car wasn't well suited for overnight use. Unfortunately, in order to get the space he wanted, Pullman had built his car too high to get past station platforms or under many bridges. It was shunted onto a siding where it collected dust for two years.

Then, in 1865 President Abraham Lincoln was assassinated, and his cortege carrying him back to Springfield, Illinois, brought out the finest railroad equipment in the nation. The slain president's home state brought out its elaborate Pullman palace car. At great expense, workmen hastily cut down station platforms and raised bridges for the run from Chicago to Springfield. Such an impression was made on visiting dignitaries that President U. S. Grant requested to ride in a Pullman on a subsequent trip from Detroit to Chicago. Hasty changes by the Michigan Central Railroad cleared its line for the oversize car. Its surge to popularity made its name so familiar that its name is widely known despite the fact that few persons of the third millennium have ever spent a night in a *Pullman*.

Cinchona

THREE centuries ago the Countess de Chinchón, wife of the Spanish viceroy of Peru, was stricken with malaria. Cured by the powdered bark known to the Indians as *quinaquina*, she took some of the medicine with her when she returned to Spain. Initially called "countess bark," it became famous.

Linnaeus, the great botanist, affixed the species name *cinchona* to the tree that produces quinine. He was honoring the countess, but he misspelled her name.

Tawdry

OUR word *tawdry*, used as an adjective to describe anything cheap and gawdy in appearance, is a corruption of the name of Saint Audrey, the daughter of an East Anglican king who founded a convent at Ely, England. At the annual autumn fair, nuns from her convent sold a variety of lace known as "Saint Audrey's lace." Through the years, its quality declined. Common people slurred over their syllables and called it "tawdry's lace." Eventually, lace and other shoddy articles sold at the fair came to be known simply as *tawdry*.

Maudlin

ONLY slightly altered, the name of Mary Magdalene of biblical fame, has become a household word. A favorite subject of medieval artists, Magdalene was almost always painted with eyes red and swollen from weeping. So anyone of similar appearance was spoken of as a "Magdalene."

In common use the name was slurred over and capitalization was dropped. This produced the adjective *maudlin*, whose meaning gradually expanded to include the trait of effusive sentimentality.

Praline

FRENCH aristocrats of the seventeenth century vied with one another in hiring chefs who could produce culinary masterpieces. One chef's invention brought a kind of immortality to his master. He concocted a candy made of sugar-coated almonds which he named for the Count Plessis-Praslin. In time the spelling was altered to *praline*. The delicacy was transplanted to New Orleans by its French founders, who substituted native pecans, and today pralines are sold on street corners in its Vieux Carré.

Sequoia

A SELF-TAUGHT American Indian is commemorated by the name of one of the oldest and largest living things in the world. Seeing a scrap of a printed page one day, a young Cherokee in Georgia called Sequoyah was fascinated by the idea of sending messages on paper. He determined to give his people a written language and worked more than ten years to produce a phonetic alphabet for them. His syllabary is made up of eighty-six characters and brought literacy to the Cherokee Nation in 1821, which allowed them to publish their own books and newspapers.

In 1847, not long after the Indian leader's death, the botanist Stephen Endlicher named the giant redwood tree *Sequoia sempervirens*.

Doily

IN the eighteenth century a merchant named Doiley kept a linen shop in the Strand in London. Many rich and fashionable women were among his customers. For them he introduced a number of new fabrics, one of them being a thin type of woolen, light enough for summer wear. It was popular, for it was both "cheap and genteel." Known as *doily*, the fabric became a favorite throughout England.

Later, the elite of the nation began using a revolutionary device—the table napkin—and often cut doily into small pieces for such use. Besides being a term for a table napkin, *doily* is also a term for an ornamental mat.

Varnish

EARLY in the third century B.C., Ptolemy III of Egypt invaded Syria to avenge the murder of his sister. His wife offered a special sacrifice to the gods for his safe return. She cut off her long and beautiful hair and hung her locks in the temple of the war god.

The lovely tresses disappeared on the first night they hung in public view. According to legend, they were wafted to heaven, where they have been known ever since as Coma Berenices. In honor of the famous beauty, the Greeks later named a city in Libya Berenike. A flourishing paint industry developed there, and when a new type of coating was perfected, it was called Berenice. For years, says legend, its original color closely resembled the amber hair of the long-dead queen.

In medieval Latin the paint was known as *bernix*. Italians corrupted its name to *vernice*. The French changed it still more, making it *vernis*. Eventually it entered English as *varnish*—some of which has a color that's still suggestive of the hair of Berenice.

Jimmy

EVERYTHING has to have a name in order to be talked about, but it seems odd that *jimmy* should be applied to a tool used by locksmiths and burglars.

In medieval times — as now — a common masculine name was James. No matter what his real name was, a helper or apprentice was likely to be called "James" or more familiarly, "Jemmy." A later counterpart was the custom of calling a chauffeur "James" and a Pullman porter "Sam."

Every craftsman in the Middle Ages had a helper, and burglars were no exception. Beginners had to serve an apprenticeship, just as though they were learning the trade of weaver or blacksmith. Like most other assistants, the burglar's helper was often called "Jemmy."

When a short crowbar with curved ends was designed, thieves found the tool so useful that it served as a helper. Since it took the place of an apprentice, or Jemmy, the name, slightly changed to *jimmy* came to be applied to it.

Guy

ON the night of November 5, 1605, a group of Englishmen who resented the hostile attitude of the government toward Roman Catholics planned to blow up both Houses of Parliament when King James I would be present. The Gunpowder Plot was discovered, and most of the plotters were killed. Guy Fawkes was the only one who was captured and executed. Since then the English have held an annual festival on November 5, complete with fireworks, during which they burn in effigy a figure representing "the guy."

In England the word *guy* refers to a person with an odd or grotesque appearance, like the effigy. Knowing little about English history, Americans have turned the word into an informal term meaning just a man or fellow. In recent years they have included women in the definition.

Tight as Dick's Hatband

WHEN a person wishes to say that a thing fits very closely indeed, it's likely to be described as being as *tight as Dick's hatband*. Logic suggests that some famous person named Dick must have had a very tight hat. That's not quite the case.

One theory regarding the origin of the expression is that it refers to King Richard III who seized the throne in 1483. To do so he had to get rid of the rightful claimant and his younger brother, Richard's nephews. The two young boys were imprisoned in the Tower of London never to be seen again. The murder of the two princes was attributed to Richard. The usurper got his punishment when he was defeated and killed at the battle of Bosworth Field in 1485 by Henry Tudor, who became King Henry VII.

Modern historians think that Shakespeare, to curry favor with Henry's granddaughter Queen Elizabeth I, put a malevolent spin on Richard's character in his play *Richard III,* which may not be justified.

The expression *tight as Dick's hatband* is a grim reminder that the crown was too tight, or dangerous, for "King Dick" to safely wear—and others need pay heed when in an analogous situation.

Goblin

SCHOLARS are at odds concerning the origin of "goblin" as one name for a mischievous spirit. Some point to a twelfth-century literary work by Ordericus Vitalis, who mentioned Goblinus as the name of a ghost that haunted the town of Eureux. This reference, they say, created the word that was later abbreviated into today's form.

Not so according to a host of critics who point out that *gobelin* wasn't regularly used until the sixteenth century. These scholars point out that a brilliant scarlet fabric unlike anything ever seen before appeared in Paris markets around 1435. Wealthy matrons vied with one another in buying tapestries made by Gilles and Jehan Gobelin, but some of their husbands frowned on the exotic cloth. It was so much more vivid in color than any previous red material that it was rumored the brothers had sold their souls to the devil in order to learn how to make the dye.

King Louis XIV made the Gobelin establishment a royal factory. Rivals denounced the craftsmen, however, and accused them of sorcery. Sentiment against the dyers was so widespread that common people began using their name as an expression for an evil spirit. As the years passed, one letter dropped from their name and now-familiar *goblin* was formed.

Melba Toast/Peach Melba

DAME Nellie Melba, the Australia-born diva of the late nineteenth and early twentieth centuries, is responsible for two food items still popular today. *Melba toast* came about by accident when the prima donna was on a diet. She requested an order of toast when dining at London's Savoy Hotel. An assistant chef overtoasted the bread slices, provoking profuse apologies by the maître d'hôtel. However, Dame Nellie liked the thin, crisp slices so much the new creation was named in her honor.

The famous chef August Escoffier created peach Melba for a party in her honor at the Savoy Hotel in 1892. The dessert consists of a peach half topped by a scoop of vanilla ice cream, topped by raspberry sauce.

Mae West

DURING World War II the name of a glamorous actress gained a place in common speech through the inspired imagination of an unknown soldier. Dressed in his life jacket, he discovered his contour was surprisingly like that of the famous movie star. "Lookit!" he yelled to his shipmates. "Come up an' see me some time!" Howling with glee, his fellow sailors dubbed the jacket *Mae West*.

Silhouette

DURING Louis XV's reign France's financial situation became precarious, and the king appointed Étienne de Silhouette as finance

minister to try to bring some order out of
disorder. Unfortunately, the minister's
reforms proved to be very unpopular.
Stingy with expenditures, he restricted
the spending of the king himself and
also proposed estate taxes on the
nobles and a variety of other taxes
affecting almost everybody. His
tenure lasted less than nine months.

Thus the phrase *à la silhouette*
("according to Silhouette") came to
mean "on the cheap."

About that time portraits made by drawing
an outline of the person, then filling in with a
solid color became popular. These "cheap" pictures got the name of
the parsimonious finance minister and thus we have the *silhouette*.

Martinet

IN European history the last half of the seventeenth century is
called the Age of Louis XIV. The Grand Monarch, the Sun King
made things French preeminent in almost every facet of life—language, thought and literature, architecture, landscape gardening,
clothing styles, cookery, and etiquette. He personally set the pace
in public events and his methods of government, administration,
diplomacy, and war became a model for other rulers to copy.

Louis and his lieutenants completely revolutionized France's
fighting forces. They created a large standing army and reorgan-
ized the internal structure and training methods. The king
appointed Jean Martinet as Inspector General of Infantry. Martinet
accomplished Louis's goals in producing a first-rate fighting
machine, in the process causing his name to enter the language.
Martinet was so rigorous in drilling and autocratic discipline that
today anyone who refuses to tolerate questions, insists upon
uncompromising obedience, and demands absolute adherence to
forms and rules—whether in the factory, home, or with a staff of
subordinates—is called a *martinet*.

BIBLIOGRAPHY

Adams, James T., ed. *Dictionary of American History*. 5 vols. New York: Scribner's, 1940.

Alsager, Christian M., ed. *Dictionary of Business Terms*. Chicago: Callaghan, 1932.

American Heritage Dictionary. 3d ed. Boston: Houghton Mifflin, 1992.

Annual Register, The. London: Longmans, Green, 1670–1985.

Barrere, Albert M. V. *Argot and Slang*. London: Whittaker, 1889.

Bartlett, John, ed. *Familiar Quotations*. 12th ed. Boston: Little, Brown, 1948.

Blunt, John H. *Dictionary of Sects*. London: Rivingtons, 1874.

Bombaugh, C. C. *Facts and Fancies for the Curious*. Philadelphia: Lippincott, 1905.

Brand-Ellis, John, *Popular Antiquities of Great Britain*; 2 vols. London: Reeves and Turner, 1905.

Brewer, E. C., *A Dictionary of Miracles*. Philadelphia: Lippincott, 1934.

————, *Dictionary of Phrase and Fable*. New York: Harper, 1953.

————, *The Historic Note-Book*. Philadelphia: Lippincott, 1891.

————, *The Reader's Handbook*. Philadelphia: Lippincott, 1904.

Cambridge History of English Literature, The. 15 vols. Cambridge: Cambridge University Press, 1907–33.

Cambridge History of the British Empire, The. 7 vols. Cambridge; Cambridge University Press, 1919–40.

Cambridge Medieval History, The. 8 vols. Cambridge: Cambridge University Press, 1911–36.

Cambridge Modern History, The. 13 vols. (Cambridge: Cambridge University Press, 1902–12.)

Catholic Encyclopedia, The. 15 vols. (New York: Universal Knowledge Foundation, 1912.)

Chambers, Robert. *The Book of Days*. 2 vols. London: Chambers, 1869.

De Vore, Nicholas, ed. *Encyclopedia of Astrology*. New York: Philosophical Library, 1947.

Dictionary of National Biography. 66 vols. (London: Oxford University Press, 1952).

Dixon, James M., ed. *Dictionary of Idiomatic English Phrases*. London: Nelson, 1891.

Encarta World English Dictionary. (New York: Saint Martin's, 1999).

Espy, Willard R. *Thou Improper, Thou Uncommon Noun*. New York: Clarkson Potter, 1972.

Farmer, J. S. and W. E. Henley. *Slang and Its Analogues*. New York: Arno reprint, 1970.

Flexner, Stuart B. *I Hear America Talking*. New York: Van Nostrand Reinhold, 1976.

————, *Listening of America*. New York: Simon and Schuster, 1982.

Goldin, Hyman E. *Dictionary of American Underworld Lingo*. New York: Twayne, 1950.

Hastings, James, ed. *Encyclopedia of Religion and Ethics*; 13 vols. New York: Scribner's, 1928.

Hendrickson, Robert. *The Dictionary of Eponymns*. New York: Dorset, 1972.

Holt, Alfred M. *Phrase Origins*. New York: Crowell, 1936.

Little, Charles E., ed. *Cyclopedia of Classified Dates*. New York: Funk and Wagnalls, 1900.

McEwen, William A. *Encyclopedia of Nautical Knowledge*. Cambridge, Md.: Cornell Maritime Press, 1953.

Mathews, Mitford M., ed. *Dictionary of Americanisms*. 2 vols. Chicago: University of Chicago Press, 1951.

Mencken, H. L. *The American Language*. 3 vols. New York: Knopf, 1936–48.

Menke, Frank G., ed. *New Encyclopedia of Sports*. New York: Barnes, 1947.

Morris, Richard B., ed. *Encyclopedia of American History*. New York: Harper, 1953.

Morris, William and Mary Morris. *Dictionary of Word and Phrase Origins.* 2 vols. New York: Harper, 1962.

Munn, Glenn G., ed. *Encyclopedia of Banking and Finance.* Cambridge, Mass.: Bankers' Publishing Co. 1949.

Notes and Queries. (London: Bell,1810–1990).

Onions, C. T., ed. *The Oxford Dictionary of English Etymology.* Oxford: Clarendon, 1966.

Partridge, Eric., ed. *Dictionary of Cliches.* New York: Macmillan, 1940.

_____, ed. *Dictionary of Slang.* New York: Macmillan, 1938.

_____, *Origins.* New York: Macmillan, 1966.

Radford, Edwin M., ed. *Encyclopedia of Superstitions.* New York: Philosophical Library, 1949.

Runes, Dagobert D., ed. *Encyclopedia of the Arts.* New York: Philosophical Library, 1945.

Seligman, Edwin R. A., ed. *Encyclopedia of the Social Sciences.* 15 vols. New York: Macmillan, 1930–35.

Seyffert, Oskar, ed. *Dictionary of Classical Antiquities.* New York: Macmillan, 1891.

Skeat, Walter W., ed. *Concise Etymological Dictionary.* Oxford: Clarendon, 1948.

Smith, Benjamin E., ed. *Century Cyclopedia of Names*; New York: Century, 1914.

_____, ed. *The Home Book of Proverbs, Maxims, and Familiar Phrases.* New York: Macmillan, 1948.

_____, ed. *Home Book of Quotations.* New York: Dodd, Mead, 1947.

Thomas, Joseph. *Dictionary of Biography and Mythology.* Philadelphia: Lippincott, 1930.

Webster's New International Dictionary of the English Language. (Springfield, Mass.: Merriam, 1947).

Weekly, Ernest, ed. *Concise Etymological Dictionary of Modern English.* New York: Dutton, 1924.

_____, *The Romance of Names.* London: Murray, 1922.

_____, *The Romance of Words*. New York: Dutton, 1914.

_____, *Surnames*. London: Murray, 1917.

Weseen, Maurice H., ed. *Dictionary of American Slang*. New York: Crowell, 1934.

Wright, James, ed. *English Dialect Dictionary*. 6 vols. London: Oxford University Press, 1924.

INDEX

Boldface entries indicate illustrations